# THE MISER

## MOLIÈRE

*Adapted by*

## MILES MALLESON

D1048364

SAMUEL FRENCH

LONDON

NEW YORK TORONTO SYDNEY HOLLYWOOD

# THE MISER

Produced at the New Theatre, London, on January 17th, 1950, with the following cast of characters:

### (in the order of their appearance)

| | |
|---|---|
| VALERE (in love with Elise) . . . . | Michael Aldridge |
| ELISE (Harpagon's daughter) . . . . | Diana Churchill |
| CLEANTE (Harpagon's son) . . . . | John van Eyssen |
| HARPAGON (the Miser) . . . . . | Miles Malleson |
| LA FLECHE (Cleante's servant) . . . . | Paul Rogers |
| MASTER SIMON (a moneylender) . . . | Leo McKern |
| FROSINE (a scheming woman) . . . | Angela Baddeley |
| JACQUES (Harpagon's servant) . . . . | George Benson |
| 1ST SERVANT . . . . . . . | Leslie Glazer |
| 2ND SERVANT . . . . . . . | William Eedle |
| MARIANE (in love with Cleante) . . . . | Jane Wenham |
| JUSTICE OF THE PEACE . . . . . | Walter Hudd |
| CLERK TO THE JUSTICE . . . . . | Norman Welsh |
| SEIGNEUR ANSELM . . . . . . | Mark Dignam |

---

## SYNOPSIS OF SCENES

*The action of the play passes during one day in the house of Monsieur Harpagon in Paris, in the year 1668.*

### ACT I

SCENE 1.—A room in Harpagon's house. Morning.
SCENE 2.—The same. A little later.

### ACT II

SCFNE 1.—The same. Afternoon.
SCENE 2.—The same. Early evening.

# THE MISER

---

## ACT I

### SCENE 1

SCENE.—*A room in the house of* MONSIEUR HARPAGON *in Paris. The morning of a day in the year* 1668.

*The setting is simple and formal. A backcloth depicts a large ornate fireplace* C. *with windows* R. *and* L. *of it giving views of a garden. There are single wings* R. *and* L., *with exits above and below them. A plush upholstered settee with a high back, stands at an angle* R.C. *An armchair to match stands* L.C., *with a stool close to and* L. *of it. The furniture is shabby with the decorative fringes bedraggled and torn. Two heavy gilt chandeliers hang* R.C. *and* L.C.

(*See the Ground Plan at the end of the Play.*)

*When the* CURTAIN *rises,* ELISE *is seated on the settee at the* R. *end of it. She is a beautiful girl in her early twenties.* VALERE, *about the same age, is kneeling* L. *of her, clasping her hand, and gazing into her eyes.*

VALERE. Then you'll marry me, you'll marry me, you will ?
ELISE (*rising*). I will—I will.
VALERE (*rising ; fervently*). My darling. My beautiful. My love. (*He takes her in his arms.*) Elise.

(ELISE *sighs deeply.*)

What a sigh. And at this moment. When you've made me the happiest man in the whole wide world. Why do you sigh ? and so deeply ?
ELISE (*breaking down* R.). I sigh, Valere, when I think of my father. (*She turns.*) How angry he'll be : demented. There'll be paroxysms of rage. I dare not imagine what he'll say or do. And my family : how they'll disapprove. And the world. The world, too, will censure me. When I think of these things, I sigh. (*She pauses.*) But I sigh *deeply* when I remember you'll not always love me as you do now.
VALERE (*breaking* L.C. *and turning*). That's true enough.
ELISE (*breaking* C.). Valere !
VALERE (*moving in quickly to* L. *of* ELISE). I shall love you more. And more, and more. Oh my dear, suspect me of anything you will,

**1**

believe me capable of any crime—but not of that.   Not of failing you.   Never, never, never, of failing you.

ELISE.   All men say such things.

VALERE.   It's what we do that matters.   You must believe me.

ELISE.   I believe you.   How easily we are persuaded by a lover. But I believe ;   you'll love me always, and will be faithful to me. And if I were told that would be a miracle, I would reply—I still believe—in miracles.   So I'll not sigh—deeply ;   I'll just sigh.

VALERE.   But why sigh at all ?

ELISE.   My dear, if only others knew you, as I know you.   When I think of all you've done for me.   Given up—everything, forsaken your country, your home, your fortune—

(VALERE *turns and moves up* L.)

—your parents—to take service in my father's house.

VALERE (*turning*).   I left my country, true—but it can hardly be said I *left* my parents—I *lost* them.

ELISE.   Still no news ?

VALERE (*moving* C.).   Well . . .

ELISE (*moving in quickly to* R. *of* VALERE).   Valere !   News ? Good ?   Bad ?

VALERE.   Neither.   Perhaps not even news.   An old friend, who knew them well, and to whom I've given the charge of continuing the search, has sent me word.   A hint—no more—that they may be yet alive.

ELISE.   But, my dear, why didn't you tell me ?

VALERE (*easing above the armchair* L.C.).   I've been wondering . . .

ELISE.   Yes ?

VALERE (*turning*).   Whether I ought **not** to—to go myself, and follow up this hint.

ELISE.   And leave me ?

VALERE.   For the time being.

ELISE.   Oh, my dear.   (*She moves in to* R. *of* VALERE.)   Valere, this friend—you can trust him ?

VALERE.   Absolutely.

ELISE.   He can do everything that you could do ?

VALERE.   Yes.

ELISE.   Don't go.   Not till you have further word.   (*She crosses below the armchair* L.C. *to* L. *of the stool, and turns.*)   If you were to leave my father's service now, he'd never take you back.   And then how could I be with you ?   Oh, stay here, close to me—and do your best to win my father's love.

VALERE.   To win your father's love ?

ELISE.   Yes.

VALERE.   Impossible.

ELISE.   But, why ?

VALERE.   He has no love to win.   (*He moves up* C.)   No love for anything or anybody, but his moneybags.

(ELISE *sits on the stool, her back half turned to* VALERE.)

Forgive me, I have no right to speak to you so, of your father.

ELISE.	But it's true.	Only too horribly, ridiculously true— (*she turns and faces* VALERE) but how highly he thinks of *you*.

VALERE.	And how easily his good opinion has been won.	Oh yes (*he moves* C.) I'm learning quite a lot, in this rather unusual situation of mine.	I'm learning that if you want a man to think well of you, all you have to do is to make him believe that you think as he thinks ; feel as he feels—like what he likes.	Especially, you have to applaud his stupidities and—follies ; praise his shortcomings ; and, above all, flatter.	Flatter, flatter, flatter.	At every turn, in every way, and all the time.	You can't overdo flattery.	The more outrageous it is, the more they like it.	(*He pauses.*)	The most cunning, the most suspicious are deceived by it.	There's nothing so inappropriate, so far-fetched, that they won't swallow, with a dose of flattery.	(*He pauses.*)	Of course, one's own integrity may suffer somewhat ; (*he moves below the settee*) but, even so, I flatter myself that the fault lies with the flatterer, not the flattered.

ELISE (*rising*).	But, Valere, my dearest, (*she crosses below* VALERE *to* R. *of him*) why don't you seek the love of my brother ?

VALERE (*turning and facing* L.).	That's impossible, too.

ELISE (*crossing to* L. *of* VALERE, *then turning and facing him*).	Surely not ?

VALERE.	Your brother is so exactly the opposite to your father, in all he says, and does, and is.	I couldn't manage the two of 'em.	(*He pauses.*)	But your idea's a good one.	(*He pauses.*)	Why don't *you* take him into your confidence ; and tell him ?

ELISE (L. *of* VALERE *and facing* R.).	Of us ?

VALERE (*looking off up* L.).	Yes.	Here he comes.

ELISE.	I dare not.	I haven't the courage.

VALERE.	My dear, you would gain his sympathy, and *I* his help.	I must go.	(*He bows and kisses her hand.*)	I have my work to do.

(*He turns abruptly, crosses above the settee and exits quickly up* R. *Simultaneously,* CLEANTE *enters excitedly up* L.	*He is a year or so younger than* ELISE.	*He is boyish, and impetuous, and just now is in a state of great excitement.*)

CLEANTE (*moving quickly to* ELISE *and clasping her in his arms*).	Sister !	Thank God, I've found you ; and alone.	(*He leads her below the settee.*)	I want to talk to you.	I've something to say to you.	It's been on the tip of my tongue for days.

ELISE (R. *of* CLEANTE).	Then why haven't you said it ?

CLEANTE.	I dared not.	I hadn't the courage.

ELISE.	Brother !	(*She sits suddenly on the* R. *end of the settee.*)	What is it you have to say ?

CLEANTE.	So much, so much, so much.	(*He pauses.*)	Yet, I can say it in one word—love.

ELISE. Cleante . . .

CLEANTE (*quickly*). Sister, I'm in love. But before I say another word, I want you to understand that I realize I can go no further in this without the full knowledge and consent of my father.

ELISE (*in amazement*). Cleante . . .

CLEANTE (*ignoring the interruption*). I'm dependent on him. (*He pauses.*) He gave me life ; and therefore, everything. (*He pauses.*) After all, our parents are older than we are. We must always remember that. And, being older, they're beyond the clutches of passion. Their's is the cool judgement of reason. In this matter of marriage, our whole future is at stake ; obviously, for our own sakes, we should allow them, out of their so much greater experience and wisdom, to choose for us ; and abide by their decision, even when it's contrary to our own.

ELISE. Cleante . . .

CLEANTE. I'm saying all this to you, sister, to save you the trouble of saying it to me yourself— (*he moves to the stool* L.C.) because I don't propose to listen to a word of it.

ELISE. Brother !

CLEANTE. No, I've made up my mind. (*He sits on the stool.*) I mean to marry the lady I love ; and nothing you can say can alter that.

ELISE. Am I, then, so utterly lacking in sympathy ?

CLEANTE (*rising, moving to the settee and sitting on it* L. *of* ELISE). Oh no, no, no, no, no. (*He puts his right arm around her.*) But you're my sister—untouched by feelings like mine—

(ELISE *turns away from him.*)

—so cool, so sensible, so full of prudence.

ELISE. Oh Cleante ! (*She gazes out over the audience.*) Even the most sensible of us can be imprudent, thank Heaven, at least once in our lives.

CLEANTE. What d'you mean by that ?

ELISE. No matter ! (*She turns and faces* CLEANTE.) It's *you* I'd hear about. Who is she ?

CLEANTE (*rising*). Who is she ! Oh, Elise ! (*He is swept up on a rising tide of ecstasy. But there is no pose in his behaviour. He is just a very young man hopelessly in love for the first time, and completely uninhibited about it. He crosses quickly below* ELISE, *moves up* R. *of the settee, then to* C. *above it, turns and faces her.*) Her eyes ! Her hair ! Her mouth !

ELISE. Yes, but . . .

CLEANTE. So young ! So fresh ! So sweet !

ELISE. Yes, yes, but . . .

CLEANTE. Her voice ! Her laugh !

ELISE. Yes, yes, yes, but . . .

CLEANTE (*moving up* L.C.). The way she moves ! Her grace ! Her modesty ! Her charm !

ELISE.  But who is she ?  Her name ?

CLEANTE (*turning to face* ELISE).  Her name !  (*He pauses. Rapturously.*)  Mariane—Mar-i-ane.

ELISE.  Mariane.

CLEANTE (*moving to the settee and sitting on it* L. *of* ELISE).  And she lives quite close to here : with her mother.  They live alone together.  Her mother's an invalid.  And Mariane looks after her.  And with what loving care !  What tenderness !  What sympathy !  So patient !  So long-suffering !  So uncomplaining !  (*He rises and moves down* L.)  And they aren't well off.

ELISE.  No ?

CLEANTE.  No.  The father's dead ; and now they've very little money.  (*He sits on the stool* L.C.)  Elise, can you imagine anything more maddening—here we are, by far the biggest house in the neighbourhood ; everybody knows father's rolling in money.  (*He pauses.*)  I long to be able to help—if only to give the mother a few delicacies, and Mariane a few pleasures.  But because we're not allowed a single penny for ourselves, I can't give Mariane even the slightest token of my affection.

ELISE (*rising and moving quickly to* CLEANTE).  Poor Cleante !  (*She kneels at his feet,* R. *of him.*)

CLEANTE (*almost in tears*).  I'm desperate.  I'm being driven to the most ridiculous subterfuges to try and borrow money—just to have something to spend on her.  (*He pauses.*)  But it can't go on like this.  I mean to have it out with him.

ELISE (*after a pause*).  With father ?

CLEANTE.  Yes.

ELISE.  What will you say to him ?

CLEANTE (*after a pause*).  Tell him of my love ; and more, my determination to get married—if he doesn't agree, if he refuses his consent, I shall—I shall——

ELISE.  Yes ?

CLEANTE.  Do something desperate.

ELISE (*kneeling up to* CLEANTE).  Oh, what ?

CLEANTE (*rising*).  I shall, I shall—leave this house.

ELISE.  Where will you go ?

CLEANTE (*with a magnificent gesture*).  Away !  Right away !

ELISE.  And leave Mariane ?

CLEANTE.  No, no, no.  I shall take her with me.

ELISE.  And what will you live on ?

CLEANTE.  There you are.  (*He crosses below* ELISE *to* R.C. *and stands with his back to her.*)  I knew you'd make difficulties.

ELISE (*rising and moving in to* L. *of* CLEANTE'S *back*).  Brother !  My dear !  I'm not *making* difficulties.  (*She moves quickly above* CLEANTE *to* R. *of him and faces him.*)  I'm pointing them out.

CLEANTE.  I don't care, something's got to be done.  It's *insufferable*—the way he keeps us both penniless.  We have to bargain with the tradesmen for the very clothes on our backs.

HARPAGON (*off up* L. ; *shouting*). Don't stand there, gaping—
you great oaf—get along with you.

CLEANTE (*crossing below* ELISE *to* R. *of her and turning*). There
he is.

HARPAGON (*off* ; *shouting*). Out of my sight !

CLEANTE (*moving up* R.). Who's he shouting at ? (*He moves up*
R.C. *and looks off up* L.) My own servant ! (*He turns to* ELISE.)

(ELISE *moves below the settee, then to* R. *of it.*)

Sister, we must join forces against him.

(*There is a loud racket off up* L., *and* HARPAGON'S *voice is heard uttering
indistinct threats.*)

ELISE (*marching above the settee to* R. *of* CLEANTE *and shaking hands
with him*). Agreed !

(CLEANTE *exits quickly up* R.C. ELISE *turns and quickly follows him
off.* LA FLECHE, *who is* CLEANTE'S *servant, enters hurriedly up* L.
*and backs to* L. *of the settee. He is followed on by* HARPAGON, *who
stands up* L., *and shakes his stick at* LA FLECHE.)

HARPAGON. You gallows bird, you ! That's what you are—a
gallows bird !

LA FLECHE (*breaking down* R. ; *muttering*). The wicked old skinflint ! (*Behind his hand to the audience.*) He's so mean !

HARPAGON. What's that ? (*He moves quickly to* R.C.). What are
you muttering—grumbling to yourself ? If you've got anything to
say, say it. Speak out.

LA FLECHE (*turning to* HARPAGON). I want to know what it's all
about. What are you turning me out for ?

HARPAGON (*threatening* LA FLECHE *with his stick*). How dare you
bandy words with me !

(LA FLECHE *dodges to* R. *of the settee.*)

(*He moves below the settee.*) Away with you ! (*He chases* LA FLECHE
*up* R. *of the settee.*) Out you go !

(LA FLECHE *runs across above the settee and armchair* L.C., *then down* L.)

(*He moves above the settee and then to* L. *of it.*) Out, out, out !

LA FLECHE (*moving* C.). Your son told me to wait for him here.

HARPAGON. Then go and wait for him in the street. Not in my
house. I won't have you in the place—not a moment longer. (*He
circles* LA FLECHE *as he speaks, first moving* R. *of him, then below him,
and finishing down* L. *of him.*)

(LA FLECHE *follows* HARPAGON *with his eyes.*)

Hanging about all day and never doing a hand's turn ; never moving ; stock-still. (*He pauses.*) Like one of the door-posts. Only
door-posts haven't got eyes. You have. And they follow me about,

everywhere.　Watching.　Trying to see if there's anything you can steal.

LA FLECHE (*facing* HARPAGON).　Steal !　A fat chance anybody has to steal anything in this house.　Everything under lock and key.

HARPAGON (*moving in close to* L. *of* LA FLECHE).　You're spying on me—that's what you're doing.　You know I've got things hidden away.　(*He claps his hand quickly to his mouth and turns away, horrified at having said too much.*)

LA FLECHE (*quickly*).　Have you ?

HARPAGON (*turning to* LA FLECHE).　What ?

LA FLECHE.　Got things hidden away ?

HARPAGON.　I didn't say so.

LA FLECHE.　Yes, you did.

HARPAGON (*breaking down* L.C.).　Oh, God forgive me—what am I saying ?　(*He turns to* LA FLECHE.)　Get out !

(LA FLECHE *turns and runs up* R.)

Come back !　(*He moves* C.)

(LA FLECHE *stops, turns and moves to* L. *of the settee.*)

What are you taking with you ?

LA FLECHE.　Thoughts.

HARPAGON.　What have you got in your hand ?

(LA FLECHE *holds out his right hand, empty.*)

The other one.

(LA FLECHE *holds out his left hand, empty.*)

Your pockets ?

LA FLECHE.　Come and see for yourself.

(HARPAGON *moves above* LA FLECHE, *and from behind him, feels and pats* LA FLECHE'S *trousers pockets.* LA FLECHE *giggles.*)

HARPAGON (*moving down* L. *of* LA FLECHE).　And your breeches ?　(*He points with his stick to* LA FLECHE'S *breeches.*)　Look at your breeches.　There's enough room in 'em to carry away half my household.　(*He crosses below* LA FLECHE *to the settee, puts his stick down on it, then bending a little, feels around the bottom edge of* LA FLECHE'S *breeches.*)

(LA FLECHE *smacks* HARPAGON, *who passes above him, then eases down* L.C.)

LA FLECHE.　Have you quite finished ?　(*Behind his hand to the audience.*)　A plague on all misers.

HARPAGON (*turning quickly to* LA FLECHE).　What's that ?

LA FLECHE (*moving in close to* R. *of* HARPAGON ; *loudly*).　A plague on all misers.

HARPAGON.　And what d'you mean by that ?

LA FLECHE. What I said.
HARPAGON. What did you say ?
LA FLECHE (*loudly*). A plague on all misers.
HARPAGON. And *who* are you talking about ?
LA FLECHE. *Them !*
HARPAGON. *Who ?*
LA FLECHE. Misers ! All misers—mean ; dried up ; terrified
—they deserve all they're frightened of. Don't you agree ?
HARPAGON (*after a pause*). You deserve a good beating. (*He
crosses to the settee and picks up his stick.*)
LA FLECHE. Oh, no, master, you flatter me—that's more than I
deserve.

(HARPAGON, *up* R. *of* LA FLECHE, *bends him over facing* L. *and raises
his stick.*)

HARPAGON. You're going to get it.
LA FLECHE. Here's another pocket. You missed it. Want to
see what's in it? (*He turns his hip pocket inside out.*) Nothing.
(*He straightens up, breaks down* L. *and turns.*)
HARPAGON (*moving to the settee*). Oh, he's being too clever for
me, I know he is. He's deceiving me. (*He sits on the settee at the*
R. *end of it.*) Oh, my good fellow . . . My dear good fellow . . .

(LA FLECHE *crosses slowly to the settee and sits on it,* L. *of* HARPAGON.)

Be a good chap and give it up.
LA FLECHE. Give what up ?
HARPAGON. What you've taken.
LA FLECHE. I tell you I've taken nothing. I've nothing in my
hands. Nothing in my pockets. (*He rises.*) Nothing in my
breeches except what's my own. So a very good day to you, dear
master. (*He moves above the settee.*) And a plague on all misers. . . .

(*He exits quickly up* R.)

HARPAGON. Thank God *he's* gone. (*He pauses.*) Although I
don't know. As long as he was here, he couldn't take anything
away with him. (*He pauses.*) Oh, what a misfortune—having so
much money about the place. Happy the man who has all his
money invested, and lives on the interest. But what investment's
really safe ? Of course, I might keep it in a bank. But I don't like
banks. Banks aren't what they're said to be. Something happens
to a bank—and then, where's your money ? Yet it's so bewildering
to find anywhere in the house. There's my strong box. But what's
a strong box ? Just bait for thieves. If thieves broke in, it would
be the first thing they'd go for. (*He rises.*) It was (*he moves slowly
up* L.C. *and looks off up* L.) a good idea of mine to bury it in the garden.
(*He moves down* L.C. *and faces the audience.*) But *was* it ?

(LA FLECHE *enters quietly up* R. *and listens.*)

People come and go in the garden, and I can't keep an eye on it, all the time. Ten thousand crowns ! In the garden !

(LA FLECHE *crosses stealthily up stage and exits up* L.)

What misery ! (*He moves to the chair* L.C.)

(ELISE *and* CLEANTE *enter up* R. *and stand silently hand in hand watching,* ELISE *below* CLEANTE.)

Was ever a man tortured by such anxieties—never a moment's peace. (*He sits in the chair* L.C., *and as he does so, sees* CLEANTE *and* ELISE). Hmm ! How long have you been there ? Come here.

(CLEANTE *moves* C.)

(*To* ELISE.) You too.

(ELISE *moves in close to* R. *of* CLEANTE, *and they again hold hands.*)

Did you hear what I was saying ?

ELISE.  No.

HARPAGON.  You must have done.

ELISE.  Indeed, no.

HARPAGON.  You didn't hear me mention (*he whispers and glances up* L.) the garden ?

ELISE.  No.

HARPAGON.  Nor ten thousand crowns ?

CLEANTE.  Ten thousand crowns !

HARPAGON (*quickly*).  I didn't mean a word of it—not a word. I mean—I—I was just thinking aloud—how good it would be if I had ten thousand crowns—in the bank, in the garden—anywhere.

ELISE (*crossing below* CLEANTE *to* R. *of* HARPAGON). Father, Cleante and I want to speak to you.

(CLEANTE *breaks to* L. *of the settee.*)

HARPAGON.  And don't you run away with the idea I meant anything else.

CLEANTE.  Father . . .

HARPAGON.  I could do with ten thousand crowns.

CLEANTE.  But, Father, everyone knows you have ten thousand crowns.

HARPAGON.  Ah ! What a wretch I am—when my own children betray me.

CLEANTE.  Betray you ? (*He breaks down* R. *and turns.*) What's wrong with saying you have ten thousand crowns when everybody knows you have ten thousand crowns—ten thousand times over ?

HARPAGON (*rising*).  Aah ! You'll be the death of me—one of these fine days. (*He crosses to* L. *of the settee and faces* CLEANTE.) Before I know where I am—I shall find myself here, in my own house, slit from top to toe—because you will go about telling people I'm made of money.

CLEANTE (*with a sharp step towards* HARPAGON).  Father

HARPAGON (*after a short pause*). Anyhow, even if it doesn't come to that, you'll be the ruin of me.

CLEANTE. Father, I want to . . . (*He breaks off.*) The ruin of you? How?

HARPAGON (*pointing to* CLEANTE *with his stick*). Well, look at you. Just look at you. Your clothes! Look at 'em. (*He moves to* CLEANTE *and circles him, touching his clothes.*) All these fiddle-faddles. Frills and furbelows and fancy knots—and all these bows. D'you want all that lot to keep your breeches up. (*He completes his circle of* CLEANTE *and stands up* L. *of him.*) There's a pretty penny there. And you've more underneath.

CLEANTE (*with a quick look at* HARPAGON). Of course.

HARPAGON. And as costly and extravagant as what I can see, I'll be bound—right thro' to your skin. Why, God bless my soul, if you were all added up as your stand there, I could buy quite a decent annuity with you. (*Suddenly.*) I never gave you the money for this get-up.

CLEANTE (*turning away*). Indeed you didn't.

HARPAGON (*with a quick step towards* CLEANTE). Then you've been robbing me.

CLEANTE (*turning to* HARPAGON). No.

HARPAGON. You must have.

CLEANTE. I've been to an old money . . .

ELISE. Ahem!

HARPAGON. Eh?

ELISE (*quickly*). He's been playing.

HARPAGON. Gambling?

CLEANTE. And lucky—winning, and spending it on clothes.

HARPAGON. If you've been winning money, you ought to put it away for a rainy day.

ELISE. Father—Cleante and I—have something to say to you.

HARPAGON (*turning to* ELISE *and peering at her*). And I've something to say to you. (*He pauses and looks from one to another.*) Well, what it is? What have you to say? What's on your mind?

CLEANTE. Well—it's—I—you see . . .

HARPAGON. Come along—out with it.

ELISE (*after a short pause*). Father, we want to talk to you about . . . (*She breaks off.*)

CLEANTE (*after a short pause*). About . . .

ELISE. About—marriage.

(*They each laugh in succession,* CLEANTE *first, awkwardly,* ELSIE *nervously, then* HARPAGON *cheerfully.*)

HARPAGON (*still laughing*). That's funny—very funny!

ELISE. Why?

HARPAGON (*after a short pause*). That's exactly what I want to talk to *you* about.

ELISE (*breaking down* L.). Oh!

HARPAGON. Eh ? Why the " oh " ? Frightened of the subject ? A great girl like you. (*He moves to* R. *of* ELISE.) At your age ! You ought to be more than ready for it. Then why the " oh "— eh ?

(*There is a pause.* ELISE *can find no answer.*)

CLEANTE (*coming to* ELISE'S *rescue*). Father, I suppose we're both a little frightened that your ideas about marriage, and ours, mightn't be quite the same.

(HARPAGON *moves to* C. *and beckons* CLEANTE *and* ELISE *to him.* CLEANTE *moves cautiously to* R. *of him,* ELISE *moves cautiously to* L. *of him. He loops his left arm in* ELISE'S *right, his right arm in* CLEANTE'S *left, and draws them in close to him.*)

HARPAGON (*confidentially*). When I've told you what I have in mind, you'll have nothing to complain of—either of you. Now— to start with—d'you happen to have heard of a family, that have only recently moved into the neighbourhood ; two of 'em—mother and daughter ?

(CLEANTE *and* ELISE *are dumfounded. There is a pause.* ELISE *finds her voice first.*)

ELISE. Yes, Father.
HARPAGON. Oh ! You've heard of 'em. When ?
ELISE (*after a pause*). Someone told me of her—of *them*—only today.
HARPAGON (*to* CLEANTE). And you—have *you* heard of 'em ?
CLEANTE. Yes, Father.
HARPAGON. Only today ?
CLEANTE. No, Father. I heard of them—some time ago.
HARPAGON. Have you *seen* 'em ?
CLEANTE. Yes, Father.
HARPAGON. You don't *know* 'em ?

(*There is a short pause.* CLEANTE *disengages his arm, breaks a little down* L.C. *and turns to face* HARPAGON. ELISE *disengages her arm and eases a little up* R.C.)

CLEANTE. Yes, Father.
HARPAGON. You *know* 'em ! Well—this is very interesting. What do you think of her ?
CLEANTE. The mother ?
HARPAGON (*impatiently*). No—the daughter.
CLEANTE. What do I think of the daughter ! (*Cautiously.*) Not unpleasing.
HARPAGON. Not unpleasing. And her looks ?
CLEANTE (*still cautiously*). Not unsightly.
HARPAGON. Not unsightly. She's the kind of girl you'd look twice at, eh ?

B

CLEANTE (*warmly*).   Oh yes—indeed.

HARPAGON.   And her manner ?

CLEANTE.   It becomes her.

HARPAGON.   Not unpleasing—not unsightly—and her manner becomes her.   Think she's a good housewife ?

CLEANTE (*enthusiastically*).   But of course.   Look at the way she does everything for her mother.

HARPAGON.   That's true enough.   In fact, if (*he raises his stick and pokes* CLEANTE *in the chest with it*) you had her for a wife, you'd think you were a very lucky fellow, eh ?

CLEANTE.   If I . . .   Oh yes, I would.

HARPAGON.   She's no money.

CLEANTE.   Oh, Father, with true love—what's money matter ?

HARPAGON (*after a pause*).   Well, I wouldn't go so far as that. But there *are* other ways of dealing with that side of it.

CLEANTE (*gripping* HARPAGON'S *right hand*).   Oh, Father !   Dear Father !

HARPAGON (*patting* CLEANTE).   Well, my dear boy, I must say this is all very satisfactory.

(ELISE *excitedly grips* HARPAGON'S *left arm.*)

I'm glad you think so well of her, very glad ; and that being so— we'll make her one of the family, eh ?

CLEANTE ⎱
ELISE ⎰ (*together ; almost jumping up and down*).   *Father !*

HARPAGON (*releasing himself and crossing below* CLEANTE *down* R.). Yes—I propose to marry her.

CLEANTE.   You propose to marry her !

HARPAGON.   That's what I said.

CLEANTE.   You !

HARPAGON.   Yes, me.

CLEANTE (*after a pause*).   But—but—who to ?

HARPAGON (*turning and facing* CLEANTE).   *Who to ?*   I said I propose to marry her.

CLEANTE.   But which ?

HARPAGON.   How which, which what ?

CLEANTE.   The mother or the daughter ?

HARPAGON.   Which d'you think ?

CLEANTE (*after a short pause*).   The mother ?

HARPAGON.   Then you're a bigger fool than I took you for.

CLEANTE (*after a pause ; breaking* C.).   But you *can't !*

(ELISE *runs above* CLEANTE *to* R. *of him.*)

HARPAGON.   And why not, pray ?

CLEANTE (*turning*).   Because . . .

ELISE (*between* HARPAGON *and* CLEANTE ; *interrupting in a composed voice*).   Cleante . . .

HARPAGON.   What's the matter with the boy ?

ELISE. I fear he's not well. Cleante, dear brother, you're ill
CLEANTE (*turning and striding up* C.). Faint ! Very faint !
HARPAGON. Faint ! Then run along into the kitchen, and get
yourself a glass of cold water—

(CLEANTE *makes a move towards* HARPAGON. ELISE *stops him with a
gesture.*)

—nothing stronger, mind.
ELISE. And lie down for a little. We can talk of this later.
CLEANTE. Yes—yes.

(*He stumbles up* R. *and exits.* ELISE *moves to the stool and sits.*)

HARPAGON (*easing* C. *and looking off after* CLEANTE). Lie down,
indeed ! Faint ! I don't know what they're coming to. Over-
dressed ! No stamina ! All their strength goes into their fiddle-
faddles. (*He pauses, glances at* ELISE, *then moves to the settee and
sits.*) Well, my dear, now you know my plan to marry again. (*As
he speaks, he takes a box of snuff from his pocket and takes a pinch.*) I
can't have you two hanging about the place—so we must get you
both married as well. I have a rich widow for your brother—a
great stroke of luck ; and for you—the good Seigneur Anselm.
ELISE (*after a pause ; looking directly at* HARPAGON). Seigneur
Anselm !
HARPAGON. Seigneur Anselm.
ELISE (*rising*). I'm obliged to you.
HARPAGON (*returning his snuff box to his pocket*). Don't mention it !
ELISE (*after a slight pause ; pleasantly*). But, saving your presence,
dear Father—(*with her back half turned to him, she curtsies*), I don't
wish to marry him.
HARPAGON (*rising and easing up* C.). And, saving *your* presence,
dear Daughter— (*he bows*) I wish that you should.
ELISE (*with her back to* HARPAGON). And begging your pardon,
my *very* dear Father—(*she steps down* R.C., *and with her back still to
him, gives a deep curtsy*) I don't mean to marry him.
HARPAGON (*moving a little down* C.). And, begging your pardon,
my *very* dear Daughter —(*he bows*) I mean that you shall. (*He
pauses.*) My dear girl, he's a wonderful match.
ELISE (*turning to face* HARPAGON). He's old.
HARPAGON. Old ? How old d'you think he is ? He's on the
right side of fifty.
ELISE. He's nearer sixty.
HARPAGON. That's what I mean. (*He pauses and places his stick
on the settee.*) You don't want to marry a young jackanapes like
your brother. Fainting and lying down all over the place. (*He
moves to* R. *of* ELISE.) You want a man in the prime of life. (*He
turns and moves up* R.) And he's immensely rich, and quite kind.
ELISE. I share your regard for him . . .
HARPAGON (*turning and moving up* C.). Very well, then . . .

ELISE (*turning her back to him*).   But I'll not marry him.

HARPAGON.   Oh, yes you will.

ELISE.   No, I won't.

HARPAGON (*moving to* R. *of* ELISE *and suddenly screaming violently at her*).   You will, you will, you will.   (*He pauses, turns and moves* C. *Quietly.*)   And this evening.

ELISE (*turning suddenly and facing him*).   This evening ?

HARPAGON.   This very evening.

ELISE.   I'll not.

HARPAGON.   You will.

ELISE.   No.

HARPAGON.   Yes.

ELISE.   You'd force me ?

HARPAGON.   I'll force you.

ELISE (*breaking down* L.).   I'd die rather.

HARPAGON (*shouting*).   Very well then, die.

ELISE.   And not marry him ?

HARPAGON.   Aah !   (*As he speaks he stumps below the settee, up* R. *of it, then above it.*)   The impudence of it !   The wickedness !   The folly.   Any other girl would jump at him.

ELISE (*moving up* L.C.).   Ask any other girl.

HARPAGON (*moving up* R.C.).   Ask anybody.

ELISE.   Very well.   (*She turns sharply towards the exit up* L.)   Here comes your new steward.   Ask him.

HARPAGON.   Valere ?

ELISE (*turning*).   Valere.

HARPAGON (*after a short pause*).   Ah now, Valere's a good fellow, a sensible fellow.   I know what he'd say.

ELISE (*after a short pause*).   So do I.

HARPAGON.   You mean you think he'd agree with *you ?*

ELISE.   I'm sure of it.

HARPAGON.   You don't know what you're talking about.

ELISE (*after a short pause*).   Father—if Monsieur Valere agrees with you, and thinks I should be obedient and marry the man you've chosen for me—then I'll acknowledge my impudence, ask your forgiveness, and marry Seigneur Anselm—this very evening.   (*She moves to the stool and sits.*)

HARPAGON.   Well, well, well.

(VALERE *enters up* L.)

Valere, come here.

(VALERE *moves to* L. *of* HARPAGON.)

My daughter and I are having a little disagreement—a little dispute —we want you to tell us which of us is in the right.   (*He moves down* R.C.)

VALERE (*after a short pause and a glance at* ELISE).   But, my dear master, there can be no doubt !

HARPAGON (*turning sharply*). What d'you mean by that ?

VALERE (*flattering*). Master ! The profound depths of your mature knowledge against the shallows of her youth and inexperience . . .

HARPAGON. Good. Very good. (*To* ELISE.) There you are, what did I tell you ? He agrees with me.

ELISE. But he hasn't heard what we're talking about.

HARPAGON (*moving to the settee and sitting*). No. But he thinks I'm right.

ELISE. Please tell him. Monsieur Valere, please listen to what my father has to say.

VALERE (*bowing to* ELISE). At your service— (*he bows to* HARPAGON) and yours, master.

HARPAGON. Well, now—listen to this. You know the good Seigneur Anselm . . .

VALERE. The old gentleman who lives in the big house at the other end of the town ?

HARPAGON. Well—yes—he lives in the big house at the other end of the town—a most worthy gentleman.

VALERE. So I have heard. Your judgement of him does you credit.

HARPAGON. Well, the good Seigneur proposed to me, that he should marry my daughter.

(*There is a long pause.* VALERE *is taken aback and looks from* HARPAGON *to* ELISE.)

VALERE. Marry your daughter !

HARPAGON. You're surprised ? (*To* ELISE.) He's surprised ! So was I—quite taken aback, but of course I accepted. (*He pauses.*) And now the young baggage says she'll have none of it. Did you ever hear anything so outrageous ?

VALERE (*with a very urgent sincerity*). No, no, never. I never heard anything so outrageous.

HARPAGON (*to* ELISE ; *overjoyed*). What did I say ?

VALERE (*with a step forward*). I can hardly believe my ears.

HARPAGON. He can hardly believe his ears. And he means it. You can hear it in his voice. Don't you ?

VALERE. I do. I do. Indeed I do.

ELISE. Does Monsieur Valere really think I should obey you in this, and marry Seigneur Anselm ? I'd hear it from his own lips.

HARPAGON. Very well, you shall. Go on. Tell her. Tell her. Plainly. In your own words.

ELISE (*rising*). Yes, Monsieur Valere. Plainly. In your own words. (*She pauses.*) And choose your words with care. (*She moves to* L. *of* VALERE.) For I have promised my father that if you think he is right—I will marry Seigneur Anselm—*this evening*.

VALERE (*after a short pause*). This evening !

HARPAGON. This evening. Now, young man. Let's hear you.

VALERE (*to* ELISE). Well, of course—as I've said—there can be no denying that your father must be right.

HARPAGON. He knows what he's talking about.

VALERE (*to* HARPAGON). Yet—at the same time— (*he eases a little to* L. *of the settee*) it might be said—in a kind of way—

(HARPAGON *looks sharply at* VALERE.)

—that your daughter is right, too.

(ELISE *eases in to* L. *of* VALERE.)

HARPAGON. My daughter is right, too ! We can't *both* be right. Don't be a dam' fool.

VALERE. Well—she might, perhaps, say that you were going a little fast.

HARPAGON. Eh ?

VALERE. Too fast for *her*. *Your* vision being so much finer and quicker in perception than hers, she has not (*to* ELISE) as yet, (*to* HARPAGON) that *certainty* that makes for unhesitating assent. (*He bends down a little towards* HARPAGON.) Whereas, given a little more time . . .

HARPAGON. Impossible. No time to spare. (*He leans towards* VALERE. *Confidentially.*) There's something about the offer that makes it unique. If he takes her at once, he takes her without a dowry.

VALERE. Without a dowry !

HARPAGON. I thought that 'ud take the wind out of your sails. I thought that 'ud rumple your feathers. Without a dowry !

VALERE. Why then—I must say . . .

HARPAGON. You see, there's nothing more to be said.

VALERE. Nothing !

HARPAGON. Nothing !

VALERE. Altho' she might perhaps say that marriage being a life-long affair, and her (*he moves above the settee, then behind it*) whole happiness or unhappiness for the rest of her life depending on it—

(ELISE *moves above the settee.*)

—and taking into consideration the great disparity in their ages . . .

HARPAGON. Without a dowry !

VALERE. Yes, of course—that's unanswerable. (*Unseen by* HARPAGON, *he gives* ELISE *a quick embrace.*)

HARPAGON. Right as usual, my dear Valere—unanswerable.

VALERE (*after a pause*). Though, of course, she might answer that there might be *some* fathers who would consider their daughter's happiness (*he eases to* R. *of the downstage end of the settee and leans over the back of it as he speaks*) rather than what they could save on them ; who would shrink from sacrificing them to a bank balance ;

who might even desire for them—all the deep joy, the inner content, the peace of mind that only a successful marriage can bring.

HARPAGON.　Without—a dowry.

VALERE (*easing up* R.).　But it must be a marriage of love. (*Behind the settee, he holds* ELISE *in his arms as he speaks.*)　Love—that unfolds and grows through the years, like a great tree—with its roots so deep that all the winds of misfortune may blow upon it, and only give it new vigour.

HARPAGON.　Yes, yes, yes.

(VALERE *and* ELISE *break.*)

That's all very well.　I know all that.　But he's in a hurry.　And we must make use of that.　He wants immediate possession . . . (*He breaks off and listens for a moment.*)　What's that ? ˘

VALERE.　What's what ?

HARPAGON (*rising*).　In the garden—a noise—didn't you hear ?

VALERE.　No.　I heard nothing.

HARPAGON.　A dog barked—I may have imagined it.　You didn't hear it ?

VALERE.　No.

HARPAGON.　You are sure ?

ELISE.　I heard it distinctly.

HARPAGON.　I thought so.　(*He moves up* L.).　That means there's someone in the garden.　I *won't* have people in the garden.　Excuse me.　Stay here.　I'll be back.

(*He exits quickly up* L.)

ELISE (*moving quickly down* C.).　Valere, don't you realize that if you agree with my father, I shall be married this evening—to someone else.

VALERE (*moving quickly below the settee to* R. *of* ELISE).　If I hadn't agreed with him, I should have been dismissed on the spot.　As it is, here I am—to prevent it.

ELISE.　How ?

VALERE.　We'll escape from this marriage, together—into our own.　We'll run away.　If your trust in me, and love, are enough.

ELISE.　Need you ask ?　(*She throws her arms around his neck.*)

VALERE (*putting his arms around her*).　Then let's thank God this has happened.　(*He kisses her.*)　My dear, my dear.　(*He glances up* L. *as he hears* HARPAGON *returning. Loudly.*)　My dear young woman (*he hastily releases himself from the embrace*) you ought to thank God—

(HARPAGON *enters up* L. *and stands watching them.*)

—this has happened.　(*He pushes* ELISE *to her knees.*)　Down on your knees, my girl—and thank God that your future husband is such a man as he is, wanting you so much that he'll not wait a moment longer than he need.　(*He looks up.　To* HARPAGON.)　Oh pardon, master, that I should talk to your daughter in this way. My feelings carried me away. (*He eases down* R.)

HARPAGON (*moving* C.). Oh, go on, go on, my boy. Don't mind me. Say what you like to her. Tell her exactly what you feel. (*He moves to* L. *of* ELISE.) And you—you wouldn't listen to *me*—perhaps you'll listen to *him*.

ELISE. Oh I *will*, Father—I will. (*She rises, moves to the settee and sits at the* R. *end of it.*) Never shall I forget what Monsieur Valere has just said to me.

HARPAGON. Splendid—splendid. Well, I have to go and make the arrangement with the good Seigneur. Valere, I leave her in your charge.

VALERE. Monsieur Harpagon, I may have to be a little—familiar with her.

HARPAGON (*easing down* L.). As familiar as you wish.

VALERE. Very well. (*He moves to* ELISE *and takes her right hand in his left.*) Now, young lady, into the next room, if you please.

(ELISE *rises.*)

And I'll come with you. (*He moves* C., *passing* ELISE *across to* R. *of himself as he does so. To* HARPAGON.) She might try to run away.

HARPAGON. Run away !

VALERE (*half turning his back to* HARPAGON, *holding* ELISE *in front of him and looking at her*). Never fear. *I'll* take care of *that*. (*He draws her up* C.) I won't let her out of my sight. (*To* ELISE.) In you go.

(ELISE *turns, moves quickly above the settee and exits up* R. VALERE *follows her quickly off.*)

HARPAGON (*easing* C. *and looking off after them*). Strange how I've taken to that young fellow. Never argues ; never contradicts. Always agrees with me. So *right*-minded ! *Such* a comfort— (*he moves up* L.) such a comfort.

*He exits up* L. *as—*

*the* CURTAIN *falls.*

## SCENE 2.

SCENE.—*The same.  A little later.*

When the CURTAIN *rises, the stage is empty for a moment, then* LA FLECHE *enters stealthily up* L. *At the same time,* CLEANTE *enters stealthily up* R.

CLEANTE (*moving above the settee*). Hey ! You ! Where have *you* been ? Didn't I tell you to wait for me here ?

LA FLECHE (*crossing down* R.). That's right. You did. And I *was* waiting—till your father came. Master—that father of yours !

Accused me of stealing ; and wanted to beat me. So I didn't wait.

CLEANTE (*moving down* C. ; *urgently*). How are things going ? It's more urgent than ever now. You won't believe it, but since I saw you last, I've discovered my own father is my rival.

LA FLECHE. Your what ?

CLEANTE. My rival.

LA FLECHE. What in ?

CLEANTE. Love.

LA FLECHE. I don't believe it.

CLEANTE (*moving up* C.). I told you you wouldn't, but it's true.

LA FLECHE (*easing down* C.). The old scoundrel ! What's he want with love ? A high rate of interest ? He's too old to take *any* interest. Did you tell him ?

CLEANTE. What ?

LA FLECHE. That you're rivals.

CLEANTE. Heavens, no. That would only have made matters worse. (*He moves down* R.) I nearly gave it away though—it was such a shock. (*He moves in to* R. *of* LA FLECHE.) But how are things going ? Have you any news for me ?

LA FLECHE. Oh, yes. I've news for you.

CLEANTE. Well ?

LA FLECHE. It's an unkind world, master, for anyone who wants to borrow money.

CLEANTE. Why, aren't we going to get it ?

LA FLECHE. Oh, yes, we shall get it—that old scamp of a go-between, that Master Simon, says he's working day and night for us—that's what he says ; and you'll be pleased to hear you've completely captivated him. Such a *charming* young man ; such good looks, with such good manners—and a lot more nonsense of that sort.

CLEANTE. But are we going to get the money ?

LA FLECHE. Oh, yes. We're going to get the money—on conditions.

CLEANTE. Did you meet the man who's actually lending it ?

LA FLECHE. Did I *what ?* Oh, no. It's not as simple as *that.* These things aren't carried on above-board in that fashion. No. They have to be wrapt in mystery. The man who's lending the money takes just as much care as you do to remain unknown. But you're to meet him this afternoon, at somebody else's house, and he's to learn from your own lips your name and security.

CLEANTE (*sitting on the settee*). My father's name ; my mother's will. Security's all right. Nothing to worry about there.

LA FLECHE. No. Nothing to worry about there.

CLEANTE (*after a pause*). Then what *are* we worrying about ?

LA FLECHE (*taking a document from his pocket*). Here are the conditions, which, I gather, our mysterious benefactor dictated, himself, to Master Simon—to be shown to you, before we go any further.

CLEANTE. Read them.

LA FLECHE (*reading with difficulty*). " Provided always that the lender is satisfied with the security— "

CLEANTE. He will be. Nothing wrong about that.

LA FLECHE. No. Nothing wrong with that.

CLEANTE (*after a pause*). Go on.

LA FLECHE (*reading*). " —then a good and exact bond shall be drawn up by an accredited notary."

CLEANTE. That's reasonable. Nothing to be said against that.

LA FLECHE. No. Nothing to be said against that.

CLEANTE. Go on.

LA FLECHE (*reading*). " In order not to burden his con-science—"

CLEANTE. His *what* ?

LA FLECHE (*moving in to* L. *of* CLEANTE *and indicating the word in the document*). Con-science.

CLEANTE. Conscience.

LA FLECHE. Conscience. (*He reads.*) " —the lender does not intend to charge more than five and a half per cent."

CLEANTE. Five and a half ! But *that's generous*. There's nothing to complain of in *that*.

LA FLECHE. No. There's nothing to complain of in that.

CLEANTE. Go on.

LA FLECHE (*reading*). " But, in consideration of the fact that the said lender has not, for the time being, in hand the said sum in question, and in consideration of the fact that the said lender is therefore compelled to borrow the said sum from another source, and at the rate of twenty per cent—"

CLEANTE (*rising ; startled*). Twenty per cent ?

LA FLECHE (*reading hastily*). " —it is hereby agreed that the said first borrower shall pay this interest in full and without prejudice to the rest, since it is only to oblige the said borrower that the said lender has himself to borrow the said money."

CLEANTE (*crossing below* LA FLECHE *to* L.). God in heaven ! That makes over twenty-five per cent. What Arab, what Jew, what Turk, is this ?

LA FLECHE. No, master, just French.

CLEANTE (*crossing angrily to* R.). Twenty-five and a half per cent. But what can I do ? I must have the money. I need it desperately.

LA FLECHE. That's exactly what I told 'em.

(CLEANTE *turns quickly and looks sharply at* LA FLECHE.)

Shall I go on ?

CLEANTE (*sitting on the settee*). Go on.

LA FLECHE (*reading*). " Of the fifteen thousand francs asked, the lender can only pay down half the amount."

CLEANTE (*rising quickly*). What's this ? Only half— (*he slowly resumes his seat*) what about the other seven thousand odd ?

LA FLECHE (*reading*). " In lieu of the remaining seven thousand, five hundred, the said borrower is requested to take various goods

and chattels, as per the accompanying memorandum. Item—a
four-poster bed with three posts, and an antique commode to
match."

CLEANTE. Antique—commode !

LA FLECHE (*reading*).  " Item—a large walnut dining table, with
five well-turned legs—the sixth unfortunately missing." (*He
pauses.*)

CLEANTE. What am I to do with it ?

LA FLECHE (*reading*).  " Item — three old-fashioned muskets,
guaranteed quite harmless, but most picturesque, with three forks
for them to stand on."

CLEANTE. Three forks !

LA FLECHE. But—quite harmless. (*He reads.*)  " Item—a brick
furnace—with two retorts, very handy for those who make a hobby
of distilling. Item — a lute from Bologna, with all its strings—or
nearly all. Item — a draught board and the game of Goose, very
useful for passing the time when one has nothing better to do . . ."

CLEANTE (*rising and crossing below* LA FLECHE *to* L.). Stop !
That's enough.

LA FLECHE. There's only one more. (*He reads.*)  "A lizard skin,
stuffed with hay, over three feet long."

CLEANTE. What ?

LA FLECHE. Over three feet long. (*He reads.*)  "A delightful
curio for hanging on a wall. All the above-mentioned reduced by
the good-will of the said lender to seven thousand, five hundred
francs." (*He folds the document and replaces it in his pocket.*)

CLEANTE (*moving in to* L. *of* LA FLECHE).  May his good-will choke
him. The thief ! You wait till I get my hands on him. (*He points
up* L.) Take me to him now—at once.

LA FLECHE. But, master, I don't know who he is.

CLEANTE. Then take me to the go-between—this Master Simon.
(*He turns up* L.)

LA FLECHE (*catching hold of* CLEANTE'S *arm*). You can't go out
like that. (*He passes* CLEANTE *across to* R. *of himself.*)

CLEANTE. And why not, pray ?

LA FLECHE. Master, when you want to borrow money, you've
got to *look* well-off. Your hat, your stick, your cloak.

(CLEANTE, *followed by* LA FLECHE, *exits hurriedly up* R. *A moment
later,* HARPAGON *enters up* L., *followed by* MASTER SIMON.

HARPAGON (*moving* C.).  And who is he—this young fellow ?

SIMON (*moving to* R. *of* HARPAGON). A young man, Monsieur
Harpagon, very badly in need of money, and who will agree to
*almost* any terms that you care to impose.

HARPAGON. Wants money badly, eh ? That's good. (*He sits in
the armchair* L.C.) But the risk, Master Simon. Any risk ?

SIMON (*moving in to* R. *of* HARPAGON). He was very highly
recommended.

HARPAGON.  His family ?

SIMON (*after a short pause*).  I've no doubt a very good one.

HARPAGON.  Yes.  But is it good for the money—that's what I want to know ?   If the father's rich, what's the boy want money for ?  Doesn't sound right to me.

SIMON (*poking* HARPAGON *in the ribs*).  His servant assures me you'll be satisfied on every point when you meet him.

HARPAGON.  But, so far, you don't know the name or the circumstances of this young client of yours.

SIMON.  That you shall hear from his own lips.  But I *do* know that the family's immensely rich.  The mother's dead, and the father very old and decrepit.  (*He again pokes* HARPAGON.)  Indeed, the young man's more or less given his word that the father'll follow his poor dead wife before very long.

HARPAGON.  Good.  That's something.  Well, if the poor young man's really in need of money, it behoves us to do what we can to help, eh, Master Simon ?   After all, there's pleasure—with profit— in helping the needy.

(CLEANTE *and* LA FLECHE *enter up* R. *and stand above the settee.*)

SIMON (*taking a document from his pocket*).  Your part of the agreement.   (*He hands the document to* HARPAGON.)

HARPAGON (*taking the document*).  Ah !   (*He studies it eagerly.*)

LA FLECHE.  Eh !   But there he is—Master Simon.

CLEANTE.  Simon !

(SIMON, *hearing his name, turns and sees* CLEANTE *and* LA FLECHE.)

SIMON (*moving to* L. *of* CLEANTE *and taking hold of his left arm*).  Well, I never expected to see *you* here.  You're in a great hurry, aren't you ?   I'm sure I don't know how you found out . . .

CLEANTE.  Found out ?

SIMON (*leading* CLEANTE *down* R.).  No matter, no matter.  I don't see there's any great harm done—and now you *are* here, we can settle the whole business on the spot.  (*He turns, and moves* R.C.   *To* HARPAGON.)  Monsieur.

HARPAGON (*looking up from the document*).  Eh ?

SIMON.  Allow me to present my young client, of whom I've been telling you.  (*He turns to* CLEANTE.)   And this, my dear young man, is the gentleman who is so generously ready to oblige us.

(CLEANTE *and* HARPAGON *glare at each other.*)

HARPAGON (*rising ; to* SIMON).  *Who* did you say this was ?

CLEANTE (*to* SIMON).  *Who's* this ?

HARPAGON (*to* SIMON).  Is *this* your young charming client ?

SIMON (*moving to* CLEANTE).  That's right, that's right—such a clever young fellow.

CLEANTE (*to* SIMON).  And is *this* my generous benefactor ?

SIMON (*moving to* HARPAGON *and tapping his right arm*).   Up to any amount—such benevolence.

HARPAGON (*hitting* SIMON's *hand with the document*).   So !

(SIMON *eases up* C.)

CLEANTE.   So !
HARPAGON.   You !
CLEANTE.   You !
HARPAGON.   You—the young rascal in want of money, and trying to borrow it.

CLEANTE (*moving in to* R. *of* HARPAGON).   You—the moneylender —at twenty-five and a half per cent.

(LA FLECHE *eases down* R.)

HARPAGON.   And you ready to pay it.   You'd have ruined me.
CLEANTE.   A lot of worthless junk for seven thousand francs.
HARPAGON.   And your father old and decrepit and about to die. Have you no moral principles ?

(SIMON *eases down* L.)

CLEANTE.   Moral principles !
HARPAGON.   Yes—haven't you heard of 'em ?
CLEANTE.   Not in this house.
HARPAGON (*glaring into* CLEANTE's *face ; indignantly*).   How can you hold up your head ?
CLEANTE.   How can you look me in the face ?
HARPAGON.   Look you in the face ?   I don't *want* to look you in the face.   Out of my sight.
CLEANTE (*turning and moving up* R.).   Gladly !
HARPAGON (*shouting after* CLEANTE).   Aren't you *ashamed* . . . ?
CLEANTE (*stopping and turning*).   Yes, I am—
HARPAGON (*moving up* C.).   I'm glad to hear it.
CLEANTE.—of *you* !

(*He turns abruptly and exits up* R.   LA FLECHE *exits down* R.)

HARPAGON (*with a move as if to follow* CLEANTE).   Aah !   (*He changes his mind, stops and turns to* SIMON.)   A nice mess you've made of it.
SIMON (*moving* C. ; *heartbroken*).   Monsieur !
HARPAGON (*moving to* SIMON *and giving him the document*).   Here's your agreement.   Take it.   And never, never accept him as a client again.   Borrowing money !   I won't have it in my family.   (*He moves slowly to the settee.*)   Take care of that—or no more commission from *me*.
SIMON.   Monsieur !
HARPAGON.   That's enough !   Go away.
SIMON.   Monsieur . . .

HARPAGON.  Go away.
SIMON.  Monsieur !
HARPAGON (*sitting on the settee*).  *Go away !*

(SIMON, *almost in tears, turns and exits sadly up* L.  HARPAGON *takes out his snuff box and becomes engrossed in taking his pinch of snuff.* FROSINE *enters cautiously up* L., *unseen by* HARPAGON.  *She moves stealthily up* L. *of the settee, is about to touch him on the shoulder, but changes her mind and coughs.*)

FROSINE.  Ahem !  Monsieur Harpagon . . .
HARPAGON (*looking up ; startled*).  What are you doing here ?
FROSINE (*with a curtsy*).  Come to see you.
HARPAGON.  Why ?
FROSINE.  You told me to.
HARPAGON.  Did I ?
FROSINE.  You know you did.
HARPAGON.  Oh yes, of course.  How did you get here ?
FROSINE.  Thro' the garden.
HARPAGON.  Who told you to come thro' the garden ?
FROSINE.  You did.  You said, " Don't come to the front door."
HARPAGON (*after a pause*).  Oh—er—how's it looking ?
FROSINE.  What ?
HARPAGON.  The garden.
FROSINE.  Lovely.  Very bright.  Very quiet.
HARPAGON.  Quiet.  Eh—good.  Anybody about ?
FROSINE.  Only the gardener.
HARPAGON.  What's he doing ?
FROSINE.  Digging.
HARPAGON.  What for ?
FROSINE.  How should *I* know ?  It's what gardeners do, isn't it ?
HARPAGON.  Where's he digging ?
FROSINE.  Among the currant bushes.
HARPAGON (*rising suddenly*).  Aaah !  (*He moves quickly up* L., *speaking over his shoulder.*)  Wait here.  Want to see you.  Back in a moment.

(*He exits hastily up* L.  LA FLECHE *enters up* R.  FROSINE *sits on the settee.*)

LA FLECHE (*moving* C.).  What's he gone off for ?
FROSINE.  After his gardener—and the poor old wretch is half-dead with overwork already.
LA FLECHE.  Half dead he may be, but he's in my way.  I've got a bit of digging to do myself.
FROSINE.  Digging—you ?
LA FLECHE.  Mm !
FROSINE.  You're up to something.
LA FLECHE.  Down to something more like.  What are you up to in these parts ?

FROSINE (*rising*). What I'm always up to. (*She moves to* LA FLECHE.) Living by my wits.

(LA FLECHE *kisses her.*)

The only thing I ever got for nothing was a little cunning, at my birth ; and the only thing I ever acquired for myself, was a little skill in using it—which I do, whenever I can.

LA FLECHE. As best you can.

FROSINE. As often as I can.

LA FLECHE. Doing business with the master, eh ?

FROSINE. From which I hope to pick up a little something for myself.

LA FLECHE. When you say—a little something, I presume you mean money.

FROSINE. What else ?

LA FLECHE. What you pick up in this house won't make your arms ache.

FROSINE. There are some things the meanest of men will pay for. (*She takes a mirror from her handbag.*)

LA FLECHE (*glancing off* L.). We shall see. Old Harpagon *is* the meanest of men.

(*There is a short pause while* FROSINE *looks in her mirror.*)

FROSINE (*replacing the mirror in her bag*). I've done him a great service.

LA FLECHE (*moving slowly down* L.). Oh, and I daresay you'll be thanked for it. But thanks are words—they cost nothing. Even so, there's one word you'll never hear from him. The little verb— to give. I give—he's never learnt to say it.

(FROSINE *moves to* LA FLECHE *and links her left arm into his right.*)

He's so mean he won't even give you good morning—he'll lend it to you. (*He pauses.*) I'm no great philosopher—but I see what I see and tho' he never parts with a sou, he's the poorer for it.

FROSINE. Then it's *my* cunning against *his* meanness.

LA FLECHE. If you were half as cunning as he's mean, you'd own half France.

(*They stroll arm in arm to the settee and sit,* FROSINE L. *of* LA FLECHE.)

The very *sight* of anyone who he thinks is going to ask for money gives him the convulsions ; and the *sound* of anyone asking for it— it's like a knife in his guts—agony. (*He kisses her, then glances up* L.) Here he comes. (*He rises quickly and moves behind the settee.*) I'm off. I'll share what you can get out of him. (*He leans over the back of the settee and kisses her, then moves to the exit down* R.) And I shan't bother to come back to collect it.

(*He exits quickly down* R. *as* HARPAGON *enters up* L.)

HARPAGON (*moving to the armchair* L.C.). I've sent him home.
Given him a few days off. The poor old chap. He's getting on,
y'know. Couldn't bear to see him digging all over the place. (*He
is about to sit.*)
FROSINE (*rising ; suddenly*). Monsieur Harpagon . . .
HARPAGON (*turning to her*). Yes ?
FROSINE. Monsieur Harpagon . . .
HARPAGON. Well, what is it ?
FROSINE (*moving* C.). You are the most remarkable man. Never
have I seen you looking such a picture of health.
HARPAGON (*pleased*). Really ? (*He sits in the armchair* L.C.)
FROSINE. Your complexion so clear, your eye so bright—
altogether so spry ; many a young man of twenty-five, I've seen
looking older than you.
HARPAGON. Ah, these days the young ones are the old ones—
fainting, and lying down all over the place. (*Something in him sud-
denly wilts.*) But for all that, you know, I've seen sixty.
FROSINE. What's sixty to a man of your age ?

(*There is a short pause. There is something pathetic in* HARPAGON'S
*wilting.*)

HARPAGON. I sometimes feel I could do with twenty years. I
sometimes wish I was twenty years younger.
FROSINE. What rubbish ! (*She crosses below* HARPAGON *to the
stool.*) A man of your calibre, with your virility, lives to be a
hundred.
HARPAGON. You think so ?
FROSINE. I'm sure of it. (*She sits on the stool.*) Give me your
hand. (*She takes* HARPAGON'S *left hand in her right, and studies it.*)
Yes, here it is. What a line of life ! Not a break in it— (*she turns
his hand over*) and it goes on for ever. If they want to get rid of you,
they'll have to put you to sleep. (*She pauses and again studies his
palm.*) And I can tell you this—you'll bury your children, and your
children's children. (*She releases his hand.*)
HARPAGON. I only hope you're right. And now, what have you
got to report ? How are things going ?
FROSINE. How can you ask ? I tell you, I've never undertaken
anything that I haven't carried thro' to a successful conclusion.
And match-making is my speciality. I began with a talk with the
mother. I told her how her daughter had caught your eye as you
sat at your window, as she passed by in the street—and how greatly
the girl pleases you ; and how you desire her in marriage.
HARPAGON. And what did she say ?
FROSINE. She was overwhelmed—at your condescension. And
when I told her that you wish her daughter to be present, here,
tonight, in your house, on the occasion of your daughter's marriage,
she willingly gave her consent.
HARPAGON. Yes—I *have* to give this supper tonight to the

Seigneur ; can't get out of it ; and I thought it would be a good opportunity to have Mariane here—there's always too much to eat on these occasions, and a lot left over.

FROSINE (*to the audience*). A generous thought !

HARPAGON. Yes, but, look here—have you talked to the old lady about a dowry, eh ?

(FROSINE *rises, crosses below* HARPAGON *to* C., *and takes a pencil and paper from her handbag.*)

She ought to make some effort to give her daughter *something*. A man doesn't marry a wife without anything to go with her, just for herself. It's unreasonable—not right—goes against my conscience. I doubt whether I ought to.

FROSINE (*turning to* HARPAGON). But she will.

HARPAGON. Will what ?

FROSINE. Bring you something.

HARPAGON. Bring me what ?

FROSINE. Five thousand crowns.

HARPAGON. Five thousand crowns ! But this is the first I've heard of it. *What* a girl ! What a *sweet* girl ! I can hardly wait. (*Anxiously.*) There's no mistake ?

FROSINE. There's no mistake—she eats only salads.

HARPAGON. Eh ?

FROSINE. Occasionally a little cheese, perhaps, and an apple or so.

HARPAGON. What *are* you talking about ?

FROSINE. None of your elaborate meals, your costly dishes. No. For years past she's been used to such a sparse diet that they wouldn't be good for her. Well, meal by meal, day by day, (*she writes some figures on the paper*) that mounts up ; say five crowns a day—that's close on two thousand a year.

HARPAGON. Yes, but . . .

FROSINE. And she's used to very simple clothes ; and takes great care of them ; never buys any new ones ; she'll be satisfied with what she's got.

HARPAGON. Ah, but will she ? Will she ?

FROSINE. A word from me, and she will. I can persuade her. If I were to tell her the simple style—the things she *has*—suit her best ; that, with those she caught you, and with those she'll keep you ; but that if she dresses up in a whole lot of silks and satins and velvets and fineries—

HARPAGON. Oh !

FROSINE. —then she'll be just like any other woman of society— one of many in your mind, and she'll lose you. (*She moves above* HARPAGON *to* L. *of him.*) Think what that means— (*she writes some figures on the paper*) another two thousand at least. Four thousand so far.

HARPAGON. Yes, but . . .

C

FROSINE. And then she's been very well brought up—she has a real horror of gambling.

HARPAGON. I should hope so.

FROSINE. Yes, but many young women of her age and class nowadays—most of 'em—play regularly and recklessly. (*She crosses below* HARPAGON *to* c.) I know a girl—not unlike Mariane to look at, same age, same background, lost four thousand last year. Four thousand! (*She writes some figures on the paper.*) Well, make it a quarter of that. There's another thousand for you ; which makes up the five thousand. (*She hands the paper to* HARPAGON.) And that's quite a lot of money. (*She moves to the settee and sits.*)

HARPAGON (*momentarily impressed*). Yes, quite a lot. (*He pauses, then rises and moves* c. *Suddenly his voice runs crescendo up the scale of indignation.*) God Almighty! What's all this about? Are you mocking me? D'you expect me to give you (*he tears the paper in pieces*) a receipt for something I haven't had? What d'you take me for?

FROSINE. A wise man.

HARPAGON. Eh?

FROSINE. But you disappoint me.

HARPAGON (*moving to* FROSINE). Disappoint?

FROSINE. I can understand the ordinary man in the street, an ordinary business man—even a *good* business man—talking like that. But you, (*she rises*) Monsieur Harpagon : you, who have such an *immense*, (*she crosses below* HARPAGON *to* R.C.) almost *cosmic*, grasp of these things ; who can look upon a balance sheet with the eye of a philosopher ; who knows the innermost meaning—the ultimate significance—of debit and credit : that *you* should fail to realize that by marrying this girl, you're five thousand crowns better off than if you married anyone else.

HARPAGON. I'd be very much better off if I didn't marry at all. I know that. And yet I've set my heart on her. (*He pauses.*) You take me for a wise man—in your heart of hearts, d'you think I'm an old fool?

FROSINE. Monsieur!

HARPAGON. Do you?

FROSINE. Monsieur, I should only think you a fool if you were foolish enough to think so yourself.

HARPAGON (*breaking* R. ; *bitterly*). But there *are* those who might think I'm—I'm a bit on the oldish side.

FROSINE. None that matter.

HARPAGON (*refusing to be comforted*). Oh, I don't know. There's the girl herself—*she* matters, I suppose, in this, in a way. Won't *she* think I'm too old?

FROSINE. Indeed no.

HARPAGON. Has she seen me?

FROSINE. No.

HARPAGON (*hopelessly*).  Well, (*he sits on the settee, at the* R. *end of it*) there you are !

FROSINE.  You can put all such fears right out of your head. (*She moves to* HARPAGON.)  She doesn't *like* young men.  She has an unconquerable aversion to them.  She has no patience with them.  She says they think of nothing but themselves.  But older men— they have an understanding of the past—an appreciation of the present, and a design for the future—gifts that only the years can bring.  (*She pauses.*)  Youth she finds insipid.  Age excites her by its very—maturity.  Only a few weeks ago, she was contracted to be married . . .

HARPAGON (*alarmed*).  Was she ?

FROSINE.  But on the very day of the marriage she broke it off when the bridegroom was able to sign the covenants without spectacles.  She has no heart, she says, for a nose that doesn't wear specs.

HARPAGON (*doubtfully*).  It all sounds a little unusual.

FROSINE.  She's an unusual girl.  (*She sits on the sofa,* L. *of* HARPAGON.)  She has, in her room, a few—but very beautiful— engravings.  And of whom ?  Of Adonis ?  Of Apollo ?  Of the youthful and god-like Paris ?  No !  But of the *aged* Priam, King of Troy ; of Nestor, *ancient* sage of Greece ; of *blind* Homer ; and the *bearded* Sophocles.  So, you see, you have nothing to fear.  Especially, as I've told you, I've never seen you looking so young.

HARPAGON (*anxiously*).  Not too young ?

FROSINE (*quickly*).  No, no, no, just right.  Let's have a look at you.  Get up.

(HARPAGON *rises perkily*.)

Take a few steps.

(HARPAGON *braces himself and takes a few stiff steps to* C.)

What poise !  What ease !  I do believe you could still dance.

HARPAGON (*enthusiastically*).  Why not ?  Why not ?

(FROSINE *hums a tune.  Thus encouraged,* HARPAGON *does a little dance, which finds him short of breath and brings on a fit of coughing.*)

Yes—there's nothing much wrong with me—except a touch of gout and this cough.

FROSINE (*rising and moving* R. *of* HARPAGON).  Oh, but Monsieur, that only completes the picture—you cough so gracefully.

HARPAGON (*clapping his hand to his right hip and tottering to the armchair* L.C.).  Well, I must say— (*he collapses into the chair*) it all sounds very satisfactory.

(FROSINE *moves in to* R. *of* HARPAGON.)

(*He pats her hand.*)  And I'm sure I'm very much obliged to you.

(*They both laugh.*)

FROSINE (*laughing throughout the speech*).   Don't mention it.   To have had the privilege of being able to render you so great a service, has made me very happy.

HARPAGON.   And I'm sure I'm very happy to have been able to afford— (*he winces at the word*) to afford you such happiness.   (*He glances off, contemplating escape.*)

FROSINE (*interpreting the glance*).   And now, Monsieur, the time has come . . .

HARPAGON.   The time ?   (*He takes his watch from his pocket and glances at it.*)   Goodness gracious me !   (*He rises, crosses below* FROSINE *to* L. *of the settee and turns.*)   I'd no idea it was so late.   I must be getting along.   (*He starts to move up* L.)

FROSINE (*intercepting him at* C.).   Monsieur, d'you understand ? I've striven so hard in your service, that the young woman you desire is all eagerness to meet you.

HARPAGON.   I'm delighted to hear it.   I'm sure I owe you a great deal.

FROSINE.   Ah, you *do*, Monsieur.   You *do*.   On your behalf, I've devoted all my time, all my energies ; yes, and all my money—and God knows, I'd little enough of that.

HARPAGON.   Dear, dear, dear.   Such devotion !   Such a capacity for helping others !   Really, I almost envy you.   (*He crosses quickly below the stool to* L. *of it.*)   Sorry I can't stay—

(FROSINE *moves above the armchair* L.C., *and intercepts* HARPAGON *up* L.)

—a little matter of business.   (*He turns about and moves below the stool to* C.)

FROSINE (*turning and moving quickly above the armchair to* C.). Monsieur, for these last few weeks, I've more or less *lived* at their house.   I've had to find excuses for going there so continuously.   I took them little presents.   (*She takes a bundle of receipts from a pocket in her petticoat and waves them at him.*)   A succession of presents ; and not such little ones.   No.   On several occasions, I took them out for a drive ; or to dinner, or to the play.   Monsieur, I've spared neither myself, nor anything that I own.

HARPAGON.   And I've told you—I don't know how to thank you.

FROSINE (*after a pause*).   It's not your thanks I want !

HARPAGON.   Indeed !   Oh well, of course, if you don't *want* to be thanked—there's no more to be said.   (*He turns and moves below the settee to* R. *of it.*)   A *little* matter of business did I say ?

(FROSINE *moves quickly above the settee and intercepts* HARPAGON *up* R.)

Most important matter.   (*He turns about and moves below the settee to* L. *of it.*)   Several important matters.

FROSINE (*moving quickly above the settee and intercepting* HARPAGON, L. *of it*). Monsieur, you must listen. (*She pushes* HARPAGON *down on to the settee. Coarsely.*) Sit down ! (*She pauses, then standing over* HARPAGON, *resumes in her normal voice.*) I've so filled her ears with your virtues, your uprightness, your good faith, your honour, your *generosity* . . .

HARPAGON. Yes, that's all very well—but I'm afraid you may have *overdone* it a bit.

(FROSINE *suddenly raises her voice to a shrill scream, and puts on an act to soften* HARPAGON'S *heart and loosen his purse-strings.*)

FROSINE. Overdone it ! *Overdone it !* Yes, I have. Not for you. No. But for myself. Yes—there you are—with your bride-to-be so eager that she can hardly wait for the marriage to be fulfilled —and here am I—I who have brought this about— (*she goes down on to her knees at his feet*) without a sou left in the world—not a sou. Oh, Monsieur, can you accept such great happiness at these hands, (*she covers her face with her hands*)—

(HARPAGON *also covers his face with his hands.*)

—and see the owner of them starve ? (*She peeps through her hands at* HARPAGON *to judge the effect of her act.*)

HARPAGON (*peeping through his hands at her ; embarrassed and hesitating*). Er—well, of course—looked at like that. (*He rises.*) I *do* realize— (*he extends a hand to* FROSINE *and assists her to rise*) there's no doubt—I'm—I'm very much in your debt. (*He takes a purse from his pocket, fumbles in it, extracts a few coins and rattles them.*) Yes—very much. (*He pauses and looks at the coins.*) Good heavens ! I never paid the gardener ! I've only just enough here.

(FROSINE *makes a grab at the purse and money.*)

(*He quickly returns the coins and purse to his pocket, dodges* FROSINE, *and almost runs up* L.C.) Oh, what's to become of me, what's to become of me.

(FROSINE *runs after him, but he exits quickly up* L.)

FROSINE (*up* C.). Become of you ! Become of you ! May your body shrink to the size of your soul and be swept on to the floors of hell—a sizzling speck of dirt. (*She moves down* C.) So much for you. But I've not done with him yet—oh no—not by a long chalk. (*She pauses.*) Now, let me see, what next ? Yes—I have to fetch Mariane, and bring her here, to the party. I don't envy her the first sight of him—but I *do* envy her his fortune. And when *that's* hers, I'll get my share of it.

*She curtsies, turns and exits up* L. *as—*

*the* CURTAIN *falls.*

# ACT II

## Scene 1

SCENE.—*The same.  Afternoon.*

*When the* CURTAIN *rises, the stage is empty.  After a moment,* HARPAGON *enters quickly down* L.  *He carries a small sheet of paper on which he has noted the arrangements for the party.*

HARPAGON (*as he enters ; calling*).  Master Jacques.  (*He crosses and calls off down* R.)  Master Jacques.  (*He turns, crosses and calls off up* L.)  Master Jacques.

(JACQUES *enters down* R.)

JACQUES.  Yes, master.
HARPAGON (*turning and moving* R.C.).  Those two good-for-nothings—are they about ?
JACQUES.  Waiting for you.
HARPAGON.  Fetch 'em in.

(JACQUES *exits down* R.  *The* 1ST *and* 2ND SERVANTS *enter down* R. JACQUES *follows them on and remains standing down* R.  *The* 1ST SERVANT *moves up* R. *of* HARPAGON, *the* 2ND SERVANT *moves* L. *of the settee.*)

Now then, come along.  Come on in.  (*He taps his paper.*)  I want to give you your orders for the party this evening.  You two have to look after the drinks—hand the glasses round.  (*To the* 2ND SERVANT.)  But don't go running at people every time you see an empty glass—or think they look thirsty.  No, let 'em ask.  And don't hear the first time.  Let 'em ask again—keep on asking. (*To* JACQUES.)  Master Jacques.
JACQUES.  Yes, master ?
HARPAGON.  That rascally son of mine—do you know where he is ?
JACQUES (*moving in down* C.).  Shall I fetch him, master ?
HARPAGON.  Yes, tell him to come here at once.

(JACQUES *turns, runs below the settee, then towards the exit up* R.)

(*He calls.*)  Master Jacques.
JACQUES (*stopping and turning*).  Yes, master.
HARPAGON.  And Monsieur Valere.  Ask him if he'd be kind enough to step this way.
JACQUES.  Yes, master.

(*He runs off up* R.)

1ST SERVANT.  Shall we serve in our aprons, master, or without ?

HARPAGON. I don't know.  Let's have a look.  Take 'em off.

(*The* 1ST *and* 2ND SERVANTS *remove their aprons.*)

Yes.  That's better.  Serve like that.  Take care not to soil your liveries.

2ND SERVANT.  Soil 'em, master !  Look here.  (*He indicates the front of his livery.*)  There's a great black stain all down the front o' mine.  Lamp oil.  Been there for years.  Can't get it off.

1ST SERVANT (*moving in to* R. *of* HARPAGON).  And I've got a large hole in me breeches, behind.  Saving your presence, they can see my . . .

HARPAGON (*quickly*).  Hold your tongue.  (*He pauses as he moves about the* 1ST SERVANT *and surveys him from behind.*)  Oh yes, so they can.  (*He moves down* C.)  Well, you'll have to keep your backside to the wall, that's all.  (*He turns to the* 2ND SERVANT.)  And you can walk about in the middle of the room, with your tray in front of you.  (*He demonstrates with his paper.*)  So.  Hide the stain.  (*He moves down* L.C. *and turns.*)  And keep a bucket of water handy—when a bottle's half empty—fill it up.

(CLEANTE *enters up* R., *and crosses below the* 1ST SERVANT *to* HARPAGON.)

(*To* CLEANTE.)  What do you want ?

CLEANTE.  You sent for me.

HARPAGON.  No, I didn't.

CLEANTE.  Yes, you did.

HARPAGON.  Did I ?  Ah, yes.  (*He refers to his notes.*)  When the young woman I'm going to marry comes to this house for the first time, be careful how you behave yourself.

CLEANTE.  Careful, Father ?

HARPAGON.  Yes.

CLEANTE.  Behave myself ?

HARPAGON.  Yes.

CLEANTE.  What d'you mean ?

(VALERE *enters up* R.)

HARPAGON.  What I say.  (*He pushes* CLEANTE *up* L.C.)  Out of the way.  (*To* VALERE.)  Ah, there you are, Valere.

(CLEANTE *moves above the armchair, then down* L.  VALERE *crosses below the* 1ST SERVANT *to* HARPAGON.  JACQUES *enters up* R. *and moves down* R.)

Good of you to come.

CLEANTE.  But—Father, why shouldn't I behave myself ?

HARPAGON.  Don't ask me.  How should I know ?  But when a man remarries, his children are usually very unpleasant about it.  And I won't have it.  No sour looks !  Give her a welcome.  Look as if you were pleased to see her.

CLEANTE. I can't say, Father, that I'm overjoyed she's to be my step-mother ; but, that I shall be pleased to see her—I can promise you that.

HARPAGON. Well, mind you are.

CLEANTE. And, Father . . .

HARPAGON. That's all. Make yourself scarce—all of you. I'm busy.

(VALERE *waves dismissal to the* 1ST *and* 2ND SERVANTS, *who exit up* R. CLEANTE *exits up* L.)

HARPAGON (*moving down* C.). Now, Master Jacques, *your* orders —and I've left you to the last.

(VALERE *moves to the stool and sits.*)

JACQUES (*moving in to* R. *of* HARPAGON). One moment, master. Are you speaking to your cook, or your coachman—for I'm both.

HARPAGON. I know that.

JACQUES. And which are you speaking to ?

HARPAGON. I'm speaking to *you*.

JACQUES. Yes, master, but I should like to do this properly. Do you speak to me as cook or coachman ?

HARPAGON. Cook.

JACQUES. Very good, master.

HARPAGON (*turning to* VALERE). Now, Valere—

(JACQUES *turns and exits quickly up* R.)

—I shall want your advice, if you'd be so good. (*He turns.*) Master Jacques . . . Hullo, where is he ? Where's he gone to ? (*He calls.*) Master Jacques.

(JACQUES *runs on up* R. *He wears a large white chef's cap, and is tying on a white apron.*)

What's all this ?

JACQUES (*moving to* R. *of* HARPAGON). Your cook, master— awaiting orders.

HARPAGON. Well—I'm giving supper to some friends.

JACQUES. I've heard so. I could hardly believe my ears.

HARPAGON. Can you give us something good to eat ?

JACQUES. I can, I can—indeed I can. Only give me the money to buy . . .

HARPAGON. Money, money, money. Why will everybody talk to me about money ? That's what it always comes to. The only word in their mouths, the only thought in their heads.

JACQUES. Oh, but master—my dear master, that's not *fair*. Not *just*. If you want me to cook you a dinner, I must have the food to cook. And to get the food, I have to buy it ; and to buy it, I must have money. Stands to reason. (*To* VALERE.) Doesn't it, master Steward ?

VALERE. No, Master Jacques, it does *not*. Anybody can produce plenty of food with plenty of money. It takes the great cook—the real artist, to make a banquet out of nothing.

JACQUES. Nothing !

VALERE. Well, practically nothing.

HARPAGON (*turning to* VALERE). Ah, Valere, Valere—what wisdom ! (*He shakes* VALERE *by the hand.*) Invaluable ! Such a grasp of *essentials*.

JACQUES (*moving above the armchair* L.C. *to* L. *of* VALERE). Oh, well, if you know how to make a dinner without anything to cook, (*he removes his cap and plants it on* VALERE's *head*) you do it yourself.

HARPAGON (*sitting in the armchair* L.C.). Don't be silly. Now, what shall we want ?

JACQUES. Ask *him*. (*He moves above the armchair towards the exit up* R.) *He's* the magician in this house.

(VALERE *removes the cap and hands it to* HARPAGON.)

HARPAGON. Master Jacques !

(JACQUES *sulkily turns and moves to* R. *of* HARPAGON.)

What shall we want ? (*He returns the cap to* JACQUES.)

JACQUES (*moving to* L. *of the settee ; grudgingly*). How many are there to be ? (*He puts on the cap, takes a small slate and pencil from his apron pocket and prepares to make notes.*)

HARPAGON. Ten.

JACQUES (*writing*). Ten.

HARPAGON. But have enough for eight.

JACQUES (*writing*). Eight.

HARPAGON. If there's enough for eight, there's enough for ten.

VALERE. How true.

HARPAGON. Eh ?

VALERE. I said—" how true ".

HARPAGON. Oh, yes, of course. (*To* JACQUES.) Make it seven —to be on the safe side.

JACQUES (*writing*). Seven.

HARPAGON. Well, what shall we want ?

JACQUES (*writing*). Well—we must begin with a tureen of soup.

HARPAGON. That's all right. Thick, filling soup—plenty of beans in it.

JACQUES. A good rich soup.

HARPAGON. Yes—no, not rich.

JACQUES (*writing*). And then, a roast.

HARPAGON (*in horror*). A roast !

JACQUES (*writing furiously ; enthusiastically*). And then some pies delicious game pies.

HARPAGON. Pies !

JACQUES. And various cheeses—and fruits.

HARPAGON. Cheese and fruits !

JACQUES. And several unusual dishes on the side.

HARPAGON (*rising*). No, no, no. (*To* VALERE.) Stop him. You must deal with this. This man'll cook me to death.

VALERE (*rising and crossing to* L. *of* JACQUES). Good master Jacques, (*he takes the slate from* JACQUES) you must realize that Monsieur Harpagon, out of the goodness of his heart, has asked his friends here to *enjoy* themselves.

(HARPAGON *eases down* L.)

The first requisite of enjoyment is—good health. And the greatest menace to good health is overeating. Any doctor will tell you that. (*He eases* C.) To invite people to sit down to a table overladen with a plethora of food is little better than murder ; the act of a culinary assassin. Now, good master Jacques, never must you forget the old saying—" we must eat to live—not live to eat ".

HARPAGON (*moving in to* L. *of* VALERE *and putting his right hand on* VALERE'S *left shoulder*). Oh, beautiful, beautiful ! What is it ? " Eat to live ; not live to eat." (*He eases down* R.C.) I'll have that engraved over my dining-room in letters of gold.

(VALERE *looks sharply at* HARPAGON.)

Well—that look like gold.

VALERE (*giving the slate to* JACQUES). There's no need for you to worry yourself about your supper party, Monsieur Harpagon. I'll see to all that. (*He moves above the armchair* L.C. *to* L. *of it*.)

HARPAGON. Good. Very good. Now—about getting the girl here. Do you think I ought to send the carriage for her ?

JACQUES. Excuse me, master.

HARPAGON. *What* is it ?

JACQUES. You wish to talk to your coachman ?

HARPAGON. About the carriage . . .

JACQUES (*moving quickly up* R.). One moment, master.

(*He exits up* R.)

HARPAGON (*turning to* VALERE). What d'you think ? Send the carriage ? Might be a good thing—just for once. (*He sits in the armchair* L.C.)

(JACQUES *enters up* R. *He wears a battered top hat and carries a long whip.*)

JACQUES (*moving* C.). About the carriage ? (*He cracks the whip.*)

HARPAGON. I want you to get it out, give it a clean.

JACQUES. Delighted.

HARPAGON. And the horses . . .

JACQUES. Impossible.

HARPAGON. Why ?

JACQUES. Not fit to go out.

HARPAGON. Why shouldn't they be fit ? What's wrong with 'em ? They never do any work.

JACQUES. They never get anything to eat. I know—with us humans—the less you do, the more you eat ; but, with the poor beasts, they'd rather do more work and get more food. (*He pauses.*) They get nothing. Except what I give 'em, myself—out of my own mouth, as you might say. I'm *fond* of 'em. I love 'em. (*He pauses.*) They're my best friends. It's hard to see your best friends starve.

VALERE (*to* HARPAGON). In any case, master, we shall want him in the kitchen. It's not far, I'll drive them myself.

JACQUES (*moving down* R.). Just as you please. And I'd sooner they died under *your* hand than mine.

VALERE. Master Jacques, you're a trouble-maker.

JACQUES. Master Steward, you are a busy-body.

HARPAGON (*rising ; to* JACQUES). Be quiet !

JACQUES (*moving* R.C., *below the settee*). I won't !

HARPAGON (*moving* C.). You won't !

JACQUES (*moving in to* R. *of* HARPAGON). I won't !

HARPAGON. You answer me back ?

JACQUES. I do !

HARPAGON. You dare !

JACQUES. I dare !

(*There is a pause as* HARPAGON *crosses below* JACQUES, *down* R.)

HARPAGON. Monstrous !

JACQUES (*following* HARPAGON *down* R.). For your own sake . . .

HARPAGON. Eh ?

JACQUES. You know, really, master, I'm quite fond of you. God knows why—but I am. I like you better than anyone.

HARPAGON. Do you ?

JACQUES. After the horses. And— (*he points to* VALERE *and whispers*) if you only knew the *truth.*

HARPAGON. The truth ?

JACQUES. About him.

HARPAGON. About him ?

VALERE (*taken by surprise ; to the audience*). What's coming now ? (*He moves above the armchair* L.C.)

JACQUES (*to* HARPAGON). How you're being deceived.

HARPAGON. Deceived ?

JACQUES. That's what I said.

VALERE (*moving* C.). Master Jacques, be careful.

JACQUES (*moving to* R. *of* VALERE). I won't be careful. I've done with being careful. I'm going to tell—the truth.

VALERE (*angrily*). Get back to your kitchen.

JACQUES. Ah, you see. He's afraid. He knows I know.

HARPAGON. Know *what ?*

JACQUES. The truth.

VALERE (*anxiously*).  Master, is this necessary ?
HARPAGON.  Let him go on.

(VALERE *breaks down* L.)

JACQUES.  Master !  That man there.

(VALERE *moves up* L.)

Your new steward—whom you engaged only the other day ;  and
already trust more than I've ever known you trust anyone ;  and
treat better, too.  If you only knew what he really is.  He's not
just a common servant—he's more than that.  He's a . . .
    VALERE (*in great agitation*).  Master Jacques !  (*He moves quickly
up* C.)  Can't you keep your mouth shut ?
    HARPAGON.  Come along, out with it.
    JACQUES.  He's a fawning flatterer—that's all he **is**.

(VALERE *smiles, breaks up* L., *and mops his face with relief.*)

*I* know.  *I* can see thro' him.  And I know if *I* could do as he does,
lie and flatter, and fawn, I should probably get double the wages
and half the work.  But *I can't*.  No, I *like* the truth.  I've a kind
of *feeling* for it, if you know what I mean.  I always tell it— (*he
moves in to* L. *of* HARPAGON) and master, oh my *dear* master, when I
hear the *lies* that he tells you—that you're good, and wise, and
generous—not a word of truth in it—it breaks my heart.  If you
only knew what people really say about you.
    HARPAGON.  And what do people really say about me ?
    JACQUES.  They say . . .  (*He breaks off and pauses.*)  No—you'd
be terribly angry if I told you.
    HARPAGON.  I shall be terribly angry if you don't.
    VALERE (*easing down* L.).  Master, you won't listen to this
impertinence.
    JACQUES (*turning and moving* R.C. ;  *to* VALERE ;  *angrily*).  And
don't *you* come butting in—filling his ears with your dishonesty.
Have you *no* respect for him ?  You know, as well as I do, he's
known as the greatest scallywag in the town.

(HARPAGON *moves to* R. *of* JACQUES.)

The meanest old skinflint in all France.  A thief ;  a usurer . . .

(HARPAGON *gives* JACQUES *a crack across the shins with his stick.*)

(*He yells.*)  Wow !
    HARPAGON.  Usurer, eh ?  (*He kicks* JACQUES' *right shin.*)
    JACQUES.  Wow !  (*He bends and rubs his shin.*)
    HARPAGON (*kicking* JACQUES' *backside*).  A thief !
    JACQUES (*straightening up*).  Wow !
    HARPAGON (*kicking him again*).  A skinflint !
    JACQUES.  Wow !  (*He falls on his face, his head to* L., *his feet to* R.)

HARPAGON.  Double wages and half the work, eh ?  From today, you get half wages and double the work.  And next time you tell me the truth, out you go.  (*He moves below* JACQUES, *faces up* L., *raises his foot to kick him, then pauses and gazes off.*)  Who's that ?  (*He runs up* C. *and looks off up* L.)  Someone in the garden.  It's that rascally man of my rascally son.  What's he doing ?  (*He calls.*)  Hi !  You !  Come away from those currant bushes.

(*He exits quickly up* L.  JACQUES *rises.*)

VALERE (*moving to* L. *of* JACQUES *and laughing kindly at him*).  Oh, good master Jacques, (*he takes hold of* JACQUES' *left arm*) I'm afraid, once again, your devotion to truth hasn't done you a great deal of good.

JACQUES (*shaking himself free ; furiously*).  What right have you to laugh at me, eh ?  (*He picks up his whip.*)  Laugh when you get a beating yourself, not when somebody else does.

VALERE (*contritely*).  Oh, no, please, please.  Don't take it to heart.  (*He moves above* JACQUES *to* L. *of the settee.*)  After all, the love of truth is a fine thing.  And if the real truth were known, of the two of us, you're the better man.

JACQUES (*turning and easing down* L. ; *muttering*).  Polite, eh ?  I believe he's frightened of me.  If I bully, he'll cringe—that 'ud make me feel a lot better.  (*He turns, swaggers to* C. *with a great show of bluster and raises his voice.*)  Now, master busy-body ; (*he pokes* VALERE *in the ribs with the butt of his whip*) master know-all ; master new broom.

VALERE (*moving in to* R. *of* JACQUES).  But no, master Jacques, I mean it.  I repeat—I respect you.  I admire you.

JACQUES.  So !  You persist.

VALERE.  Yes.

JACQUES.  You—respect me ?

VALERE.  I do.

JACQUES.  Do you ?

VALERE.  Very much indeed.

JACQUES.  You—admire me !  (*He pushes* VALERE, *suddenly and violently, in the chest.*)  None of your silly flattery with me.

(VALERE, *surprised, gives way.*)

(*He drives* VALERE *backwards to the settee in a series of pushes as he talks.*)  I'm sick of you.  (*Push.*)  Find something to do.  (*Push.*)  Paid more than any of us.  (*Push.*)  And do less.  (*He pushes* VALERE *down on to the settee and stands over him.*)  It's time you were taught a lesson.  (*He whacks* VALERE *across the shins with the whip.*)

VALERE (*rising quickly and snatching the whip from* JACQUES).  That's enough.  You go too far.  You forget yourself.  After all, you're only a—coachman.

JACQUES (*cringing*).  *And* a cook.
VALERE (*after a short pause*).  *And* a fool.  A great fool.  (*He pushes* JACQUES *in the chest.*)

(JACQUES *gives way.*)

(*He drives* JACQUES *backwards to the armchair* L.C. *in a series of pushes as he talks.*)  You have a passion for truth, eh ?  (*Push.*)  But no reverence for it.  (*Push.*)  You babble it.  (*Push.*)  You blurt it out.  (*He pushes* JACQUES *down into the armchair* L.C. *and stands over him.*)

(JACQUES *cringes.*)

And it's time *you* were taught—a lesson.  (*He pauses, then hands the whip to* JACQUES, *turns and moves down* R.)  There are times, master Jacques, when the truth is too naked to be seen, too sacred to be told, too brittle to be hammered.  Gently does it, master Jacques, tact, discretion, manipulation.  (*He laughs and demonstrates, making a gesture with the fingers of both his hands close together.*)  Manipulation !

(*He turns and exits down* R.)

JACQUES (*rising and moving* C.).  Very good, master Steward.  (*He throws the whip angrily on to the floor down* R.)  I've done with the truth.  Done with it.  But not with *you*—oh no, not with *you*.  (*He stands gazing off* R.)

(FROSINE *enters quietly up* L., *moves to* L. *of* JACQUES *and taps him on shoulder.* JACQUES *turns, startled.*)

FROSINE.  Is the old boy about ?
JACQUES (*moving down* R. *and picking up the whip*).  In the garden.
FROSINE.  Be a good soul, and tell him I'm here, with his ladylove.
JACQUES.  His *what ?*
FROSINE (*moving below the settee*).  You heard.  Get along with you.

(MARIANE *enters up* L. *and moves* C.  JACQUES, *with his eyes all the time on* MARIANE, *moves up* R., *crosses upstage, and exits up* L.)

MARIANE.  Oh, Frosine, I'm so miserable.

(FROSINE *eases up* R.C.)

How I dread this meeting !
FROSINE.  Oh, come now, my dear, it's not as bad as that.
MARIANE.  I know, now, what it must have been like to be led to the rack.  The first sight of it !  (*She moves to the armchair* L.C.)  And everybody around, eager to see one stretched in agony.  (*She sits.*)
FROSINE (*moving to* R. *of* MARIANE).  Well, of course, if you put it like that, old Harpagon isn't exactly the death I should choose.

But look me in the eyes, girl. This sudden distress isn't so much because of the old man, but of the young man you've just told me about.

MARIANE. I can't deny it. I can't. Oh, Frosine, if you were bringing me to *his* house. If it were *he* who was to be my husband.

FROSINE. And you've no idea who he is ?

MARIANE. No idea.

FROSINE. How often has he been to see you ?

MARIANE. Not often enough.

FROSINE. Did he bring presents ? Expensive ones ?

MARIANE. No.

FROSINE. None ?

MARIANE. None.

FROSINE. Then he's probably as poor as a church mouse. If you married him, he'd give you a baby—and that's about all you'd get out of *him*. But this old one—he'll die.

MARIANE But I don't want him to die.

FROSINE. He's got to. It's in the contract.

MARIANE. In the contract ?

FROSINE. Not in so many words, in black and white. But between the lines. Written, my dear, by the finger of time in invisible ink. And he'll leave you his fortune—and that *is* in the contract, and (*she moves quickly below the settee*)—

(HARPAGON *enters up* L. *and moves down to* L. *of the stool.   He wears a pair of heavy horn-rimmed spectacles.*)

—here he comes.

MARIANE (*after a hasty glance at* HARPAGON). Oh ! (*She closes her eyes and leans back in the chair.*)

HARPAGON. Ah, my dear.

MARIANE (*opening her eyes*). Ugh ! (*She gazes at him in horror.*)

HARPAGON. I'm afraid I must ask you to excuse these spectacles. But the truth is, I'm not as young as I was.

(FROSINE *eases slowly up* C.)

I'm beginning to find these things useful—especially for signing contracts.

(MARIANE *glances at* FROSINE, *then resumes her gaze at* HARPAGON.)

Of course, (*he becomes embarrassed by her stare*) I know there's no need to wear spectacles to observe your beauty. No. But, on the other hand, one *does* wear them to look at the sun. (*He laughs nervously.*)

(MARIANE *looks in stricken silence at* FROSINE.)

(*He moves behind the armchair, then above* FROSINE *to* R. *of her.*) What's the matter with her ? Why doesn't she answer ? She doesn't seem pleased to see me.

FROSINE. Shy. She's shy. (*She raps* MARIANE *surreptitiously with her fan.*) A young girl hesitates to show her deepest feelings. (*She raps* MARIANE *again.*)

(ELISE *enters up* R. FROSINE *eases above the armchair, then to* L. *of it.*)

HARPAGON (*to* MARIANE). There's my daughter.

(MARIANE *rises.*)

Come to pay her respects. (*He moves to* ELISE.) Come along, child. (*He leads her* C.) Elise, this is Mariane. Mariane, my dear, this is Elise.
    MARIANE (*with a curtsy*). So pleased.
    ELISE (*with a curtsy*). Delighted.
    MARIANE (*resuming her seat in the armchair* L.C.). I have to ask your pardon. I should have paid this visit before.
    ÉLISE. On the contrary, I'm remiss. If I'd known sooner . . .
    HARPAGON (*moving between* ELISE *and* MARIANE ; *to* MARIANE, *indicating* ELISE). Big, isn't she ? But rank weeds grow apace. (*He laughs nervously again.*)

(ELISE *eases below the settee.*)

MARIANE (*turning to* FROSINE). Detestable creature !
    HARPAGON (*moving behind the armchair* L.C. ; *to* FROSINE). What's she say ?

(CLEANTE *enters up* R.)

FROSINE. She's overwhelmed. Now she's seen you, her feelings are even stronger than she expected.
    HARPAGON (*moving down* L. *of the armchair ; to* MARIANE). Oh, my dear ; and I'm overwhelmed by your opinion of me. Ah, there's my son. (*He moves above the armchair to* R. *of it.*)

(MARIANE *turns and whispers to* FROSINE, *who is* L. *of her.* CLEANTE *eases* C.)

Come along, my boy, come along. (*He speaks out of the corner of his mouth to* CLEANTE.) Remember what I told you. (*To* MARIANE.) Mariane, my love—this is my son, Cleante.

(MARIANE, *with her eyes downcast, rises.*)

Cleante, my boy, this is Mariane.

(CLEANTE *bows.* MARIANE *gives a deep curtsy and as she does so, looks up and recognizes* CLEANTE. *Aghast and agape, she is unable to rise from her curtsy, and collapses gracefully into a sitting position on the floor.*)

MARIANE (*with a little cry*). Frosine !
    FROSINE (*dropping to the floor* L. *of* MARIANE). What is it ?

MARIANE (*speaking to* FROSINE *behind her fan*).  It's he.

(CLEANTE *moves* R. *and with his back to* HARPAGON, *whispers with* ELISE.  HARPAGON *looks anxiously from one pair to the other*.)

FROSINE.  Who ?
MARIANE.  He !
FROSINE.  No ?
MARIANE.  Yes !
FROSINE (*rising*).  My God !
HARPAGON (*moving down* C.).  What's this ?
FROSINE.  Nothing.
HARPAGON.  Nothing ?
FROSINE (*assisting* MARIANE *to rise*).  She's a little upset.
HARPAGON.  What about ?
FROSINE.  Your son.
HARPAGON.  My son !
FROSINE.  His size.  He's so grown-up.
HARPAGON (*moving in to* R. *of* MARIANE).  Oh, that's it, is it ?  Of course.  Yes.  I understand.  My grown-up children.  (*To* MARIANE.)  But that's nothing to worry about, my dear.  (*He takes her hand.*)  All the easier to get rid of.  (*He passes her in front of him to the armchair* L.C.)

(MARIANE *sits*.)

(*To* CLEANTE.)  Now, my boy—give her your welcome.  (*He eases below the stool.*)

(FROSINE *eases above the armchair* L.C.)

CLEANTE (*turning*).  What can I say ?  How can I speak to her ?  Father, may I call this young lady—Mariane ?
HARPAGON (*to* MARIANE).  May he call you Mariane ?
MARIANE (*looking at* HARPAGON).  With all my heart.
FROSINE (*moving to* R. *of* MARIANE ; *with a warning cough*).  Ahem !
CLEANTE (*stepping to* C. *and facing* MARIANE).  Mariane—Mar-i-ane !  It doesn't need my father's bidding for me to tell you how pleased I am to see you.

(HARPAGON *looks sharply at* CLEANTE.)

Pleased—is too small a word.  This room, this whole house, has changed since you entered it.  (*He pauses.*)  There are moments in our lives that live for ever.  This is such a moment.

(HARPAGON *places the stool as close as possible to* MARIANE'S *chair*.)

For me, you will always be there, as you're there now—a loveliness, unfading, as long as I have memory to contain it.
HARPAGON.  Not bad—not so bad.  (*He bends to* MARIANE.)  A bit flowery, perhaps—but not so bad.

D

CLEANTE (*violently*). But the thought of being your step-son, of having *you* for a step-mother, is not to be borne. (*He breaks down* R.C.) Unendurable ! Too horrible for words ! An outrage !

HARPAGON. What's this ? The rascal !

MARIANE (*rising ; pushing* HARPAGON *down on to the stool and taking a step to* C.). No, Monsieur. Let *me* answer him. (*Forcibly*.) Young man, please understand this—I feel as you do.

(CLEANTE *turns and faces* MARIANE.)

Exactly the same. Just as strongly.

(FROSINE *raps* MARIANE *with her fan*.)

(*She raps* FROSINE *with her fan*.) And, after hearing what you had to say, to have you for a step-son, to be your step-mother, would indeed be unendurable—not to be borne.

(FROSINE *fans herself furiously and moves up* L.)

HARPAGON (*rising and crossing below* MARIANE *to* L. *of* CLEANTE). Good, good, good ! I like a young woman of spirit. (*To* CLEANTE.) You got as good as you gave. Now—say you're sorry.

(ELISE *eases behind the settee*.)

MARIANE. No. Please. I'm glad he spoke as he did. (*She glances over her shoulder at* FROSINE.) I'm deeply grateful. (*She curtsies*.) Now I know where I am with him. (*She eases down* L.C.)

HARPAGON. We'll make him change his tune.

CLEANTE (*striding up* C.). Never. (*He turns.*) I shall never change.

(ELISE *eases up* R. *of the settee*. FROSINE *eases down* L. *of the stool*.)

HARPAGON (*moving up* C. *to* L. *of* CLEANTE). I give you just one more chance. Now then.

CLEANTE. Very well, Father. I'll change my tune. I'll say this —if I were in your place, Father, I should consider I had found the perfect wife. (*He pauses.*) I should (*he moves slowly to* R. *of* MARIANE) want no further pleasure than to please *her*—I should see no beauty in the world but hers. (*He pauses.*) To call myself her husband would be the greatest honour I could covet ; (*he kneels to* MARIANE) and to be a good one, the proudest of careers. (*He takes* MARIANE'S *hands in his.*) I should want no riches, except to see that *she* wanted nothing—counting myself the richest of men, possessing her. (*He pauses.*) Not only *I* would be wholly hers, every thought, every action ; but everything I owned, every penny piece.

HARPAGON (*moving* R. *of* CLEANTE). Hey, hey, hey, that's enough —no good overdoing it. Now you're getting ridiculous.

(FROSINE *grips* MARIANE'S *left arm and swings her away down* L. ELISE *crosses slowly up stage to* L. CLEANTE *rises. As he does so,* HARPAGON *grips* CLEANTE'S *right arm and swings him away* R.C.

CLEANTE *notices a ring* HARPAGON *is wearing and grips his right hand.)*

CLEANTE. Mariane! Have you ever seen a diamond more beautifully cut, or that sparkles more brilliantly, than this on my father's finger? (*He lifts* HARPAGON'S *hand.*)

(ELISE, *at a sign from* CLEANTE, *moves in close to* L. *of* HARPAGON.)

FROSINE. No indeed. It certainly seems to sparkle wonderfully.
CLEANTE. Seems to sparkle! But it *does*.

(CLEANTE *loops his left arm through* HARPAGON'S *right, and* ELISE *loops her right arm through his left, securing him between them.*)

And the setting—isn't it exquisite?
ELISE (*to* MARIANE). Can you see?
MARIANE (*crossing below* FROSINE *to* R. *of her*). Yes.
FROSINE. No, no, you can't.
ELISE. Of course you can't. Not properly.
CLEANTE. You must see more closely.

(ELISE *and* CLEANTE *bring* HARPAGON *down* R.C.)

HARPAGON (*under his breath to* CLEANTE). I got it for a bad debt, and it's worth a fortune.

(ELISE *pulls* HARPAGON *round to* L. *of her. As she does so,* CLEANTE *draws the ring off* HARPAGON'S *finger.*)

CLEANTE. My father wishes you to admire it. (*He holds the ring out to* MARIANE.)

(ELISE *breaks up* L.C. HARPAGON *moves above* CLEANTE *to* R. *of him, makes a grab at the ring and misses.*)

MARIANE. Indeed, it shines bright, (*she moves to* R. *of* CLEANTE) but so hard it looks—cruel.

(FROSINE *eases to* L. *of* MARIANE.)

CLEANTE (*slipping the ring on to* MARIANE'S *finger*). Not on this hand. Now see how soft and kind its light. (*He passes* MARIANE *across to* FROSINE.)

(FROSINE *passes* MARIANE *up* C. *to* ELISE, *then breaks down* L.)

HARPAGON (*grabbing* CLEANTE *and leading him down* R. ; *whispering*). Don't be a fool, boy.

(MARIANE *moves to* R. *of the armchair* L.C.)

(*He leads* CLEANTE *up* R., *behind the settee.*) Give it back—I won't have it. I won't have it. Back.
CLEANTE (*moving quickly above the settee to* L. *of it ; to* MARIANE.) My father won't have it—back. He wishes you to keep it.

HARPAGON (*moving hastily down* R., *then below the settee*).  Keep it !
CLEANTE.  You hear.  He wishes to make you a present of it.

(MARIANE *sits in the armchair* L.C.)

HARPAGON (*turning, moving below the settee, then up* R. *of it*).  I
shall go out of my mind.  (*He is so distracted he does not hear*
MARIANE'S *next remark.*)
MARIANE.  Oh no, no, no—please.  (*She takes the ring from her
finger.*)  I couldn't dream of it.  I won't accept it.
HARPAGON (*moving above the settee to* L. *of* CLEANTE *and hissing in
his ear*).  You young blackguard !  (*He crosses below* CLEANTE
*down* R.)
CLEANTE (*to* MARIANE).  Keep it—keep it.
HARPAGON (*pacing up* R., *behind the settee and down again*).  This
is outrageous.
CLEANTE (*to* MARIANE).  What did I say ?
HARPAGON (*down* R.).  Does she know what it's worth ?
CLEANTE (*aside to* MARIANE).  You don't know how you're hurting
him.
HARPAGON (*moving in to* R. *of* CLEANTE *and hissing into his ear*).
Thief, thief, thief.  (*He breaks down* R.)
CLEANTE (*easing towards* MARIANE).  He's getting desperate.
Keep it.
FROSINE.  Keep it—keep it.
MARIANE.  Shall I ?

(HARPAGON *paces up* R.)

ELISE.  Keep it.  You can give it back to him later.
FROSINE.  But not now ; we don't want him to have a fit.
ELISE.  Keep it for now—keep it.
MARIANE.  Very well.  (*She replaces the ring on her finger.*)
CLEANTE (*turning and moving above the settee to* HARPAGON).  She's
so overcome, she has no words to thank you.

(HARPAGON *glowers at* CLEANTE, *who backs away up* C.  VALERE *enters
down* R.)

HARPAGON (*moving behind the settee to* VALERE *down* R.).  I'm
upset, Valere, almost beyond endurance.  But I must pull myself
together.  I must be agreeable—yes—yes.  (*He moves below the
settee to* MARIANE *and takes her hands in his.*)  My dear, my dear.
(*The sight of the ring on her finger forces a groan from him.*)  Ooh !

(VALERE *moves up* R., *then to* C., *where* CLEANTE *is standing with*
ELISE.)

My dear, would you like to be shown over the house ?  We're to
have a little supper later, when the Seigneur comes.  I'm sorry
we've nothing to offer you just now.
CLEANTE (*moving to* L. *of the settee*).  Oh, but we have.

HARPAGON (*after a pause ; turning to* CLEANTE).  Have what ?

CLEANTE.  Something to offer.

HARPAGON.  What ?

CLEANTE.  It's all set out in the next room.

HARPAGON.  In the next room ?

CLEANTE.  Yes.

HARPAGON.  What's set out ?

CLEANTE.  Ptarmigan, quail, peaches, pineapples, nectarines, grapes, sweetmeats from Tunis, and some of the choicest wines money can buy.

HARPAGON (*aghast*).  Merciful God !

CLEANTE (*moving down* R.).  You wanted her to have a real welcome, so I ordered them, and—had them put down to your account.

HARPAGON (*moving quickly up* R.).  Put down to . . .  Oh !  Oh ! (*He stops and turns.*)  Valere, did you know about this ?  (*He grabs* VALERE.)  Choice wines !

(*He turns and exits hurriedly up* R., *dragging* VALERE *off with him.*)

ELISE (*moving quickly to* MARIANE).  Darling Mariane.

(MARIANE *rises.*  FROSINE *moves above the armchair* L.C.)

My brother has told me.  (*She leads* MARIANE *to the settee.*)

MARIANE ⎫                  ⎧ How kind you are.   I hope you'll always
         ⎪                  ⎪ be my friend, whatever happens.   It will
         ⎪                  ⎪ make—whatever happens, so much easier
         ⎬ (*together*).  ⎨ to bear.
ELISE    ⎪                  ⎪ I'm so happy to meet you ; to make your
         ⎪                  ⎪ acquaintance ; to become friends ; and
         ⎭                  ⎩ alas, to tell you how sorry I am.

(MARIANE *and* ELISE *sit on the settee,* MARIANE *below* ELISE.)

CLEANTE.  Whatever happens ?  But what *is* going to happen ? What are we going to *do* ?

MARIANE.  What *can* we do ?

CLEANTE.  We must do *something !*

MARIANE.  I'll do anything you ask ; anything you tell me.  Tell me what to do.  I know you'll ask nothing dishonourable.

CLEANTE.  Oh, if you're going to limit me like that . . .

MARIANE.  Cleante, dear Cleante—in this, I'm thinking not so much of myself, or even of us, but of my mother.   With me, she has practically nothing ; without me, nothing at all.   It was for *her* sake I agreed to this marriage.

FROSINE (*moving down* L.C. ; *approvingly*).  Spoken like a good girl.

CLEANTE (*with a step towards* FROSINE ; *bitterly*).  You got us into this.

FROSINE.  Me ?

MARIANE⎱
ELISE  ⎰ *(rising ; together).* Yes.

(MARIANE *eases below* CLEANTE, ELISE *above him.*)

CLEANTE.   Now get us out of it.
FROSINE.   I like that ! How did I know this was going to happen ? Why didn't you tell me ?
CLEANTE.   We didn't know ourselves.
FROSINE.   Then don't blame *me.*
ELISE *(moving above* FROSINE *to* L. *of her).*   But you will help them.

(CLEANTE *eases up* R. *of* FROSINE, MARIANE *moves in to* R. *of her.*)

FROSINE.   Oh, well, if there's anything I can do, I'll do it. Of course. *(She kisses* MARIANE.*)*   I'm not hard. At least, I made myself hard. *(She turns and kisses* ELISE.*)*   The good God made me soft—and His work is the better done. When I see true love, I melt, like ice before a flame. *(She moves between* CLEANTE *and* MARIANE *and turns.)*   So—let's think. *(She links her left arm into* CLEANTE'S *right, and her right arm into* MARIANE'S *left.)*   First of all, young man, *(she takes them slowly* R.C.*)* if your father gets wind of this— only a sniff of it—out you go, into the street ; *and* without a penny. *(She releases their arms.)*

(*All three turn so that* CLEANTE *is down* R., FROSINE *up* L. *of him, and* MARIANE *up* L. *of* FROSINE.)

And what then ? Of course, you could starve in each other's arms —there are worse deaths.

(ELISE *moves to* L. *of* MARIANE.)

But, as she says, there's her mother. *She* has only her memories— poor fare, at the best of times. No, it's your father, my lad, that's the trouble. *(To* MARIANE.*)* He's set his heart on you. *(She moves and sits on the settee.)*   And I don't blame him.

(LA FLECHE *enters up* L. *and moves behind the armchair* L.C. *The others, pre-occupied, do not notice him.*)

But what to do ?
ELISE *(easing up* L. *of the settee).*   If we only had some bargaining power.
MARIANE *(crossing down* R.*).*   Some hold over him.
CLEANTE *(moving below the settee, then up* R. *of it).*   Some of his money.

(ELISE, MARIANE *and* CLEANTE *hang their heads in despair.* LA FLECHE *makes signs over the back of the armchair* L.C. *to* FROSINE. *He points first to himself, then towards the exit up* L.*)*

FROSINE. Little hope of that. He would . . . (*She sees* LA FLECHE *making signs and breaks off. Cautiously.*) I'm not so sure. (*She rises.*)

(LA FLECHE *ducks behind the armchair* L.C.)

I believe I know a man who might help.
CLEANTE. Help ?
ELISE. In what ?
LA FLECHE (*standing up and speaking over the back of the armchair* L.C.). In getting—pardon the intrusion—in getting some of his money.

(CLEANTE, ELISE *and* MARIANE *move quickly and group around the armchair* L.C., *facing* LA FLECHE, CLEANTE *above it,* MARIANE *below it and* ELISE *kneeling on the seat.*)

And what's more— (*he winks at* FROSINE) I believe I know a woman who might help that man.
FROSINE. The man would want paying.
LA FLECHE. The woman would do it for nothing.
FROSINE. I think not.
LA FLECHE. No ? Twenty per cent.

(CLEANTE *eases up* L.)

FROSINE. No !

(ELISE *rises and breaks up* C.)

LA FLECHE. Twenty-five ?
FROSINE. Oh, no !
LA FLECHE. And a half ?
FROSINE (*moving above the armchair* L.C.). And the ring.
LA FLECHE. What ring ?
MARIANE (*removing the ring from her finger*). This ring. (*She hands the ring to* LA FLECHE.)
CLEANTE. Isn't that rather a lot ?

(LA FLECHE *gives the ring to* FROSINE.)

FROSINE (*moving* C. *and putting the ring in her handbag*). Think of the people you're dealing with. A human shark . . .

(MARIANE *moves up* R. *of the armchair* L.C. *to* R. *of* CLEANTE.)

LA FLECHE. A human jackdaw . . .
FROSINE. And the risk.

(CLEANTE *and* MARIANE *embrace.* LA FLECHE *crosses to* L. *of* FROSINE.)

(*To* CLEANTE.) For your father to lose his wife is one thing, but to lose his money . . .

(LA FLECHE *kisses* FROSINE *and takes her handbag from her*.)

Think of his rage. (*She takes her handbag from* LA FLECHE.) But he'll give up anything to get it back—even Mariane.
    ELISE.  Oh, Frosine !
    CLEANTE (*gazing at* MARIANE).  Oh, Mariane !
    MARIANE (*gazing at* CLEANTE).  Oh, Cleante !
    FROSINE.  Oh, you two !
    LA FLECHE (*to* FROSINE).  Oh, you beauty !
    FROSINE.  Oh, you wretch !
    ELISE (*glancing off* R.).  Oh, my goodness ! There's a certain person coming.
    FROSINE (*quickly*).  Pretend to be dancing. (*She starts to hum a tune, grabs* LA FLECHE, *and dances him down* L.)

(ELISE *dances solo behind the settee, then down* R.  CLEANTE *takes a step away from* MARIANE, *but doesn't leave go of her hand. For a moment he stands holding it and gazing at her in adoration, then he bows low over her hand and kisses it lovingly. As he does so,* HARPAGON, *followed by* VALERE, *enters up* R.)

HARPAGON (*to* VALERE).  What's this ? My son kissing his future step-mother's hand.

(CLEANTE *quickly drops* MARIANE'S *hand, who turns to face* HARPAGON. LA FLECHE *exits unobtrusively down* L.)

    VALERE.  Very praiseworthy.
    HARPAGON.  Very queer—I must see into it. (*He moves to* R. *of* MARIANE.)  Now, my dear—you want to see the house. (*He turns to* ELISE.)  Elise.
    ELISE.  Yes, Father ?

(CLEANTE *eases down* L.)

    HARPAGON.  Will you do the honours.  **And Valere—**
    VALERE.  Yes, master ?
    HARPAGON.  Will you go with Elise ?
    VALERE (*moving down* R. *to* ELISE).  Certainly, master.

(MARIANE *crosses below* HARPAGON *and joins* ELISE *and* VALERE *down* R.  CLEANTE *crosses below the armchair* L.C. *to follow them*.)

    HARPAGON.  And Cleante—
    CLEANTE (*stopping* L. *of the settee*).  Yes, Father ?
    HARPAGON.  You stop here—I want to talk to you.
    CLEANTE.  Yes, Father.

(CLEANTE *and* FROSINE *exchange a look*.)

    HARPAGON.  Now then, the rest of you—what are you waiting for ? Off you go—and Frosine, you too.

FROSINE (*crossing down* R. ; *under her breath to* CLEANTE *as she passes him*).  Be very careful—I think he saw.

(ELISE, MARIANE, FROSINE *and* VALERE *exit down* R.)

HARPAGON (*moving slowly to the stool and sitting*).  And now, my boy.  (*He pats his armchair, motioning* CLEANTE *to sit*.)

CLEANTE (*moving cautiously to the armchair*).  Now what, Father ? (*He sits*.)

HARPAGON (*after a pause*).  What d'you think of her ?

CLEANTE (*very cautiously*).  Er—what do I think of her ?

HARPAGON.  Yes.

CLEANTE.  Of Mariane ?

HARPAGON.  Of course.

CLEANTE.  Er—oh—so, so !

HARPAGON.  Eh ?  So-so.  That's all ?

CLEANTE.  Well, (*he relaxes and turns to* HARPAGON) to tell the truth, Father, frankly, I was disappointed.  Her figure is awkward ; her prettiness ordinary ;  and her manner both coy and insipid. Mind you, I wouldn't say a word against her.  As step-mothers go, I'd as soon her as anyone.

HARPAGON.  But the things you said to her ?

CLEANTE.  Oh, trifles, my dear Father, trifles—thrown off more to please you than her.

HARPAGON.  Then she doesn't attract you ?

CLEANTE.  Good heavens—no.

HARPAGON.  Not in the least ?

CLEANTE.  No.  Not in the least.

HARPAGON (*after a pause*).  A pity.  (*He rises and crosses to* C.) A great pity.

CLEANTE.  A pity, Father ?

HARPAGON (*over his shoulder*).  I'm sorry.

CLEANTE.  Sorry ?

HARPAGON (*easing to* L. *of the settee*).  Quite knocks it on the head.

CLEANTE.  What on the head ?

HARPAGON.  An idea of mine.

CLEANTE.  What idea ?

HARPAGON (*sitting on the settee, at the* R. *end of it*).  The fact is, when I saw her here in my house, face to face, I made up my mind to drop the whole thing.  But then, as I'd offered my hand to the girl, given my word, I couldn't just put her out into the street, could I ?  No—I thought I'd give her to you.

CLEANTE (*rising suddenly*).  Give her to me ?

HARPAGON.  Yes.

CLEANTE.  In marriage ?

HARPAGON.  My dear boy, what d'you think ?  Yes, of course.

CLEANTE (*moving up* C. *and turning ; after a pause*).  Father, (*he pauses*) my dear Father, for *your* sake, and to please *you*, I'll marry her.

HARPAGON. Although she's—awkward, and—ordinary, and—what was it—coy and insipid ? And she doesn't attract you. No—not in the least.

CLEANTE (*moving* C.). Out of my love for you, I'll make the sacrifice.

HARPAGON (*rising and moving to* R. *of* CLEANTE). Out of my love for you, I won't accept. (*He pauses.*) What d'you take me for ? Forcing a child of mine against his will—'tisn't in my nature.

CLEANTE. But, perhaps, Father, after we're married, love may come. They say it does happen like that.

HARPAGON (*easing to the settee*). I won't risk it ; couldn't have it on my conscience. As I say, it's a pity—but I must have her myself. (*He sits on the settee at the* R. *end of it.*)

CLEANTE (*moving to the settee and sitting* L. *of* HARPAGON). Father, I must open my heart to you.

HARPAGON (*half turned from* CLEANTE). Do, my boy, do ; that's what I want.

CLEANTE. I love her. Desperately—ever since I first set eyes on her. I want to marry her ; more than anything in the world. I was going to ask your consent to our marriage ; but, when you told me of your plan, out of my great respect for you, I held my tongue.

HARPAGON. Have you known her for a long time ?

CLEANTE. Not long.

HARPAGON. Have you been to her house ?

CLEANTE. Oh, yes.

HARPAGON. Often ?

CLEANTE. Very often ; considering what a short time I've known her.

HARPAGON. Have you told her of your feeling for her ?

CLEANTE. Yes.

HARPAGON. Does she return it ?

CLEANTE. I believe she does. But, of course, she didn't know who I was. Just now she was completely taken by surprise.

HARPAGON (*rising*). I see. (*He suddenly crosses below* CLEANTE *to* C. *and turns sharply to face him. His voice runs up the best part of an octave, into a screech.*) You young dog !

(CLEANTE *rises, startled.*)

Is there no devilry you're not capable of ? A sink of lies and deception—that's what you are. God knows where you get it from !

CLEANTE. A sink of deception ? I ?—and you've deceived me into telling you.

HARPAGON. And I won't have you poaching on my preserves.

CLEANTE. Poaching ! It's *you*—trespassing. I was there first.

HARPAGON. There first ! You'd never have been there at all if it hadn't been for *me*.

CLEANTE (*angrily*). I'll never give her up.

HARPAGON (*raising both his hands threateningly over his head*). I can't keep my hands off you.

(JACQUES *enters up* R.)

CLEANTE ⎫ (*together*). ⎧ You'd better . . .
HARPAGON ⎭　　　　　 ⎩ I can't, I can't . . .

JACQUES (*running down between* CLEANTE *and* HARPAGON, *separating them*). Hey, hey, hey—what's this? My dear old master—my good young master.

HARPAGON (*crossing below* JACQUES *and* CLEANTE *to* R.). Good? There's nothing good about him ; but he wants a good beating.

(CLEANTE *moves to* R. *of the armchair* L.C. *and turns*.)

JACQUES (*moving to* L. *of* HARPAGON). Oh, no, no. Beat me, Masters, if it'll do you any good ; but not your own flesh and blood.

HARPAGON. If you knew what had happened—you'd condemn him, without another thought. You shall judge ! I'll tell you ; and you shall be the judge between us.

JACQUES. The judge between you !

CLEANTE (*moving to* L. *of* JACQUES). I agree to that.

JACQUES. As you will, dear master—as you will. Oh, master Cleante, don't stand there, looking so fierce. (*He pushes* CLEANTE *across to* L. *of the stool*.) A little further off, my good boy—a little further off, if I'm to be the judge. There— (*he turns and moves to* L. *of* HARPAGON) while I listen to what your father has to say.

(*During the next speech,* HARPAGON *takes hold of* JACQUES' *right arm with his left hand, and walks him around the settee, first below it, then up* R. *of it, then above it, and finishing* L. *of it*.)

HARPAGON. I decide to remarry ; choose the lady ; make the arrangements—and, if you please, along comes my son, and informs me he proposes to marry the lady himself.

JACQUES. Oh dear, dear, dear. No, no, no.

HARPAGON. Oh, dear, dear, dear. Yes, *yes*, YES ! And he won't give way. No obedience. No respect. Just defiance. (*He sits on the settee*.) What d'you think of that ?

JACQUES. Shocking. He can't be serious. (*He runs around the armchair* L.C., *then down* L. *of it to* L. *of* CLEANTE.) No, master Cleante.

(*During his next speech,* CLEANTE *takes hold of* JACQUES' *right arm with his left hand, and walks him around the armchair and stool, first below them, then up* C., *then above them, down* L. *of them, finishing below the stool*.)

CLEANTE. Jacques, in the town, I meet the loveliest young woman you've ever set eyes on. I bow ; she smiles. I fall in love ; and, miracle of miracles, she loves me—and now I find my father proposes to buy her for himself. What d'you think of that ?

JACQUES. Oh, shocking, shocking, shocking. He must be joking.

CLEANTE (*sitting on the stool*). A very bad joke.

JACQUES (*crossing down* C. ; *to the audience*). *Now* what am I to do ? There's only one thing I know—the truth's no good. (*He moves to the settee and sits on it,* L. *of* HARPAGON.) Master—it's all a mistake. He says he doesn't want to marry the lady—if you'll find him someone else he can be happy with.

HARPAGON. If he'll give up Mariane, he can have anyone he chooses—anyone.

JACQUES (*rising*). Leave it to me. (*He crosses to the armchair and sits. To* CLEANTE.) Master, it's all a mistake. It's the way you behave makes him so angry. He'll let you marry the lady you love, if you'll only show him more respect.

CLEANTE. If he'll give me Mariane, my respect of him will be unbounded.

JACQUES (*rising*). Leave it to me. (*He crosses to* HARPAGON.) It's all arranged.

HARPAGON. Thank God for that !

JACQUES (*crossing to* CLEANTE). It's all fixed up.

CLEANTE. Heaven be praised !

JACQUES (*moving* C. *and looking from* CLEANTE *to* HARPAGON). There, my masters ! Gently does it, gently—tact, discretion. (*He moves down* C. *To the audience.*) They were quarrelling all for the want of a little— (*he demonstrates as* VALERE *did earlier in the Scene, making a gesture with the fingers of both his hands close together, but cannot remember the word*) er—what he said.

CLEANTE (*rising and easing down* L.) Jacques—you're a good fellow.

(JACQUES *moves in to* R. *of* CLEANTE.)

(*He takes a coin from his pocket.*) You deserve something for yourself. (*He gives the coin to* JACQUES.) Take that.

JACQUES (*taking the coin*). Oh, thank you, master. (*He gapes at the coin.*) Thank you.

HARPAGON (*rising*). Jacques ! And I, too. (*He eases down* R.)

(JACQUES *crosses to* HARPAGON *and holds out his hand.*)

I'm obliged to you. (*He puts his hand in his trousers pocket.*) You deserve a reward. I—all my life, (*he brings an extremely dirty khaki handkerchief out of his pocket*) I shall be in your debt. (*He blows his nose.*)

JACQUES. Thank you, master, thank you.

(*He turns, moves up* R. *and exits.* CLEANTE *and* HARPAGON *at opposite sides of the stage, in mutual embarrassment, take side-long glances at each other.*)

CLEANTE (*after a pause*). Father, (*he pauses and takes a step towards* c.) I must ask your—pardon—your forgiveness for my bad manners, and my bad temper.

HARPAGON (*taking a step towards* c.). Oh, that's all right, my boy, that's all right.

CLEANTE (*taking another step*). I can only say I'm very sorry.

HARPAGON (*taking another step*). And I—that I'm overjoyed to find you so reasonable, so understanding, so considerate.

CLEANTE (*taking another step*). How generous of you to overlook all my faults.

HARPAGON (*taking another step*). Oh, it's easy enough to forgive the exuberance of youth, as long as it's realized that there *is something* due to our years.

CLEANTE (*taking another step*). Indeed, indeed, yes—I promise, never in my life, shall I forget this.

HARPAGON (*moving in to* R. *of* CLEANTE). And I promise—if ever there's anything you want, just ask me, (*he puts his left arm over* CLEANTE'S *right shoulder and kisses him French fashion on the right cheek*) and you shall have it. (*He kisses* CLEANTE *on the left cheek and pats his back with his left hand.*)

CLEANTE (*over* HARPAGON'S *left shoulder*). What more can there be to ask—now that you've given me Mariane ?

HARPAGON (*after a pause*). I beg your pardon ? (*He breaks from* CLEANTE.) I don't think I quite heard. Say that again.

CLEANTE. I was only saying, dear Father—what more can I want —now you have given me Mariane ?

HARPAGON. And who, dear Son—if I may ask—said anything about giving you Mariane ?

CLEANTE. You.

HARPAGON. I ?

CLEANTE. But, of course ! Just this moment.

HARPAGON. But it was *you*, who renounced *her.*

CLEANTE. I ?

HARPAGON. But of course ! Just this moment.

CLEANTE. Most certainly *not.*

HARPAGON. *Not ?*

CLEANTE. *Never !*

HARPAGON. What's this ? You mean, in spite of all you've just said, in spite of having given me your solemn word, you're going back on it ; within a few moments ?

CLEANTE. As you're incapable of keeping a promise for more than ten seconds—yes. Yes. A thousand times yes.

(HARPAGON *suddenly slaps* CLEANTE'S *right cheek. There is a pause for a few moments as* CLEANTE *stands too surprised to speak or move, then he puts his hand to his cheek, crosses slowly below* HARPAGON *to* R. *and turns.*)

HARPAGON (*turning furiously to* CLEANTE).   Out you go !   D'you hear ?   Out !   Out of my house !   Out !

(LA FLECHE *enters quietly down* L.   *He carries a large casket-like box clasped in his arms.   It is about all he can manage ; and embarrassed by its weight, he makes violent and quite unintelligible signs behind* HARPAGON'S *back to* CLEANTE—*who stands staring, agape, at this surprising phenomenon.*)

(*Unaware of* LA FLECHE, *he continues without interruption.*)   Out ! I never want to see your face again.   Never !   I cast you forth.   I disown you.   I renounce you.   I disinherit you—d'you hear ?

(CLEANTE *continues to stare over* HARPAGON'S *shoulders at* LA FLECHE.)

You're renounced, disinherited, disowned, cast forth.   (*He pauses.*) Confound it, boy, you might listen when I'm talking to you.   (*He realizes that* CLEANTE *is staring agape, with eyes that are not focussing on him, but on something behind his back.*)   What is it ?   What's the matter ?   What have you seen ?   What are you staring at ?

(LA FLECHE, *still with the casket in his arms, exits quickly down* L.)

Something in the garden ?   (*He turns and looks up* L.)   What was it ? What did you see ?   (*He moves quickly up* C. *and looks off* L.)   Something unusual ?   Something unusual in the garden ?   You must have done.

(*He exits hurriedly up* L.   CLEANTE *watches him go and takes a few mystified steps after him.*   LA FLECHE, *still with the casket, enters down* R.)

LA FLECHE (*calling*).   Master !
CLEANTE (*turning to* LA FLECHE).   Well, what is it ?   (*He moves to* L. *of* LA FLECHE.)   What do you want ?
LA FLECHE (*mysteriously*).   Under the currant bushes !
CLEANTE.   Currant bushes ?   What *is* all this ?   What are you talking about ?   What have you there ?
HARPAGON (*off* L. ; *calling*).   Thieves !   Thieves !
LA FLECHE.   Listen.
HARPAGON (*off* L. ; *calling*).   Thieves !   Help !   Thieves !
LA FLECHE.   Quick, master—out of his way.

(*He turns and exits quickly down* R., *followed by* CLEANTE, *as* HARPAGON *enters hurriedly up* L.   *He is utterly distraught, and runs madly about the stage.*)

HARPAGON.   Thieves !   Thieves !   Murder !   Fire !   I'm finished ; I'm done for.   (*He runs down* C.)   I'm lost.   I've been robbed. Robbed, robbed, robbed.   (*He runs up* C.)   My money !   It's gone !

It's not there ! Somebody's taken it. Who can have taken it ?
Who ? Who ? Who, who, who, who, who, who, who ? (*He sobs.*)
Whooo, whooo ? (*He moves to* L. *of the settee.*) Stolen ! Stolen !
Somebody's stolen it ! Where have they gone ? (*He moves above
the armchair* L.C.) Where are they hiding ? (*He moves up* C.) They
must be somewhere ! Of course they must. Somewhere. Oh, if
I could lay my hands on 'em. (*He grips his left wrist with his right
hand.*) My hands on 'em. Oooooh ! Oooooh ! Wowh ! What's
the matter ? What's happening ? (*He moves down* C.) Something's hurting ! (*He looks at his hands.*) Oh, look. (*To the audience.*) I've got hold of myself ! (*He waggles his left hand, the wrist
still gripped.*) I've arrested myself. (*He releases his grip.*) I don't
know where I am. I don't know what I'm doing. I can't believe
it. I can't. Gone ! All gone ! Ten thousand crowns. (*He
pauses.*) Ah, my money ! My poor dear money—where are you
now ? They've taken you away from me. (*He moves to the settee
and sits*). How lonely you must be. (*He pauses.*) There's nothing
left—nothing. No more meaning in anything. No joy—no happiness—no purpose. My comfort ; my consolation ; my support—
gone. I shall never get over it—never. I shall die—I'm dying.
I'm dead. I'm buried. (*He rises.*) I don't know what I'm talking
about. (*He moves* C.) Steady, steady, steady. I must be calm—
I must keep control of myself. I must think. What can I *do* ?
That's it—what can I *do* ? (*He sits in the armchair* L.C.) Do ?
Do ? Do ? *The police* ! Of course. Fetch the police. They'll
investigate. They'll find it. They'll get it back. (*He rises.*)
Everybody in the house must be cross-examined—everybody. They
must be *made* to confess ; and if they won't, then put to the torture.
No favouritism. The whole household. All the servants ; my own
children, my son and my daughter—and me, too, if necessary. (*He
moves* C.) Now, which of 'em do I suspect ? (*He pauses.*) I
suspect 'em *all*. (*He sits again in the armchair* L.C.) As I think of
each one, I'm sure they did it. (*He suddenly claps his hands over
his ears.*) I can hear 'em laughing ! They're laughing at me.
Why ? Why are they laughing ? (*He rises.*) Because they *all* did
it. They've all taken my money. That's it. They've all got a
share of it. (*He moves down* C.) Laugh, laugh, laugh away. But
I'll be revenged. Wait. (*He moves to the armchair* L.C. *and holds
on to it.*) Wait till I fetch the police—and the detectives and the
inspectors and the superintendents ; I'll fetch 'em all—and the
magistrates, and the justices, and the judges and the hangman—with
his gallows. I'll hang 'em all ! I'll hang the whole world ! And
if that doesn't get my money back— (*he moves up* R.) I'll hang myself.

*He exits up* R. *as—*

*the* CURTAIN *falls.*

## SCENE 2

SCENE.—*The same.   Early evening.*

*When the* CURTAIN *rises, the stage is empty.   Almost immediately, the* JUSTICE OF THE PEACE *enters up* R., *followed by* HARPAGON *and the* CLERK TO THE JUSTICE.   *The* CLERK *carries a small folding stool, a note-book and pencil, and a sheaf of papers.*

JUSTICE (*as he enters ; fussily*).   You can leave it all to me, good Monsieur Harpagon, all to me.   (*He moves to* R. *of the armchair* L.C. *and turns.*)

(*The* CLERK *moves up* C., *opens the stool, sits on it, and prepares to take notes.* HARPAGON *moves behind the settee, then down* R.)

No need to get excited.   No need to get excited.   Gracious goodness me, no.   This isn't the first robbery I've had to deal with. Indeed, indeed, it isn't.   I only wish I had a hundred gold pieces for every thief I've caused to be hung.

HARPAGON.   And that's what you've to do now ; hang the thief. Catch him and hang him.

JUSTICE.   Hang him !

HARPAGON.   And quickly.   And if you can't, I'll find another Justice who can.   Every Justice in the neighbourhood must concern himself over this.

JUSTICE (*moving up* C.).   Over this !

HARPAGON (*sitting on the settee, at the* L. *end of it*).   And if, together, they can't get my money back—

JUSTICE.   Money back !

HARPAGON.   —I'll have justice on the Justices.

JUSTICE.   Justice on the Justices !   (*He backs to the folding stool up* C., *and without looking behind him, sits.   As the* CLERK *is already sitting on the stool, he sits on the* CLERK's *knees.*)   Dear, dear, dear. Irregular.   Very irregular.   No.   We must follow the usual procedure.   We must follow the usual procedure.   (*He rises.*)   Now— this missing casket.   (*He eases to* R. *of the armchair* L.C.)   What was in it ?

HARPAGON.   My money.

JUSTICE (*to the* CLERK).   His money.

(*The* CLERK *makes a note.*)

JUSTICE (*to* HARPAGON).   How much ?

HARPAGON.   Ten thousand crowns.

JUSTICE (*to the* CLERK).   *Ten* thousand crowns.

CLERK (*making a note*).   Ten thousand crowns.

HARPAGON   Ten thousand.

JUSTICE.   Ten thousand.

CLERK.   Ten thousand.

JUSTICE.   Quite a robbery !

HARPAGON.  That's what I'm telling you.

JUSTICE.  Telling you !

HARPAGON.  A terrible robbery.  The blackest in the whole history of mankind.  And if it goes unpunished, the most sacred things in Heaven and earth are sacred and safe no more.

JUSTICE (*after a short pause*).  Um—d'you suspect anyone ?

HARPAGON.  Yes.

JUSTICE.  Good.  Who ?

HARPAGON (*rising*).  Everybody.  (*He crosses down* L.)  You must put the whole town under arrest—and most of the suburbs.

JUSTICE (*moving to* R. *of the* CLERK).  Irregular.  Very irregular.  No.  (*He snatches the papers from the* CLERK.)  We must proceed in the usual way, quietly and carefully.  (*He turns the papers over, mixes them and generally gets them into an untidy mess.*)  First, sift the evidence, then collect and confirm the proofs, and then, (*he drops the papers to the floor*) seize our man.

(*The* CLERK *rises and gathers up the papers.*)

HARPAGON (*moving below the armchair* L.C.).  I can't wait.  Let's seize him first.

JACQUES (*off* R. ; *calling*).  Tie him up—tie him up !  First, slit his throat—then hang him from the ceiling.

(*The* CLERK *runs behind the armchair, then hides behind* HARPAGON.)

Give his feet a good grilling and soak 'em in boiling water.

(*The* JUSTICE *crosses below* HARPAGON *and hides behind the* CLERK.)

HARPAGON (*to the* JUSTICE).  D'you hear that ?  (*He runs up* L. *of the settee and looks off* R.)  He's got him.

(*The* CLERK *and the* JUSTICE *creep to* HARPAGON, *and hide behind him.*)

He's caught the thief.

(JACQUES *enters up* R.   *He carries a butcher's knife and steel, and wears his chef's cap.*)

Jacques has caught the thief.

JACQUES (*moving to* HARPAGON).  Oh, master—such unexpected happenings—you could never guess—into my arms as it were, out of the blue.

(*The* CLERK *and the* JUSTICE *creep above the armchair* L.C., *the* CLERK *leading, the* JUSTICE *clinging on behind him.*)

HARPAGON (*easing* C.).  Who is it ?

JACQUES (*easing to* R. *of* HARPAGON).  Who ?

HARPAGON.  Yes, who ?

JACQUES.  There's no who.

HARPAGON.  No who ?

JACQUES.  Oh, master, the most divine little sucking pig.

**E**

HARPAGON. Sucking pig ?

JACQUES. For the supper. I'm having it prepared in a special way of my own.

HARPAGON. Never mind about that now. (*He moves to* L. *of the* CLERK.) Never mind. This gentleman wants a word with you.

JACQUES (*after a pause ; looking at the* CLERK). Is he coming to the supper ?

HARPAGON (*pushing the* JUSTICE *towards* JACQUES). He wants to ask you some questions.

JACQUES. Questions ? (*He sharpens his knife on the steel during the next speech.*)

JUSTICE (*nervously eyeing the knife*). Don't be alarmed, my man.

(HARPAGON *moves above the* JUSTICE *and* JACQUES *to* R. *of the settee. The* CLERK *sits on the stool up* C.)

Nothing to worry about. No need to be nervous—whatever you've done. I'll get it out of you.

JACQUES. Whatever I've done ?

JUSTICE. Yes.

JACQUES. Well, as a matter of fact, it isn't.

JUSTICE. Isn't what ?

JACQUES. Done. Not quite. But as soon as it is, you shall have it.

JUSTICE. You must keep nothing back.

JACQUES. No. Indeed no. Why should I ? But, if it isn't enough—well—if I hadn't the money—what could I do ?

JUSTICE. Oh, so you hadn't the money, eh ? What have you done with it ?

JACQUES. Done with what ?

JUSTICE. The money !

JACQUES. What money ?

HARPAGON. The money you stole ?

JACQUES (*turning to* HARPAGON). Stole ?

HARPAGON. And if you don't give it back, I'll have you hanged.

JUSTICE (*moving above the settee to* HARPAGON). No, no, no, you mustn't say things like that.

(JACQUES *backs to* R. *of the armchair* L.C.)

You mustn't talk to him in that way. Most irregular. (*He glances at* JACQUES.) No. I can see by his face he's a truthful man. We shall get what we want out of him, without having to lock him up. (*He moves above the settee to* C. *To* JACQUES.) Now, my man, if you want to keep out of prison, all you have to do is confess. No harm'll come to you, and you'll be suitably rewarded.

HARPAGON. No—no !

JACQUES. Confess !

JUSTICE (*after a pause*). A large sum of money has been stolen. You're the only man who can know about it. Tell us all.

JACQUES (*breaking down* R.).    Stolen !   *Now* what am I to say ʄ
(*To the audience.*)    Not the truth—even if I knew it.

(*The* JUSTICE *eases up* C. *to* R. *of the* CLERK.)

But what a chance to get my own back on that steward.

HARPAGON (*moving above the settee ; to the* JUSTICE).    What's he
muttering about ?

JUSTICE.    Let him alone.    He's making up his mind to confess.
I told you he was a truthful man.

JACQUES (*turning to* HARPAGON).    Master, if you must know—it
was your steward.

HARPAGON (*after a pause*).    My steward ?

JACQUES.    Yes.

HARPAGON.    Valere !    Monsieur Valere !

JACQUES.    Yes.

HARPAGON.    The only man I thought I could trust.

JACQUES.    That's him.    He did it.

JUSTICE.    What makes you think so ?

(HARPAGON *eases behind the settee, then down* R.)

JACQUES (*easing to* L. *of the settee*).    Um ?    What—what makes me
think so ?

JUSTICE (*moving to* R. *of the armchair* L.C.).    Yes.    What makes
you think so ?

JACQUES.    I think so, because—I think so !

JUSTICE.    But you must have your reasons.

JACQUES.    Oh, yes.    I have my reasons.

JUSTICE.    What reasons ?

JACQUES.    What reasons ?

HARPAGON (*moving below the settee*).    For instance, did you see
him hanging round the place where I put it ?

JACQUES.    Yes, I did—where did you put it ?

HARPAGON.    In the garden.

JACQUES.    That's right.    (*To the* JUSTICE.)    I saw him in the
garden.    (*To* HARPAGON.)    Where did you keep it ?

HARPAGON.    In a casket.

JACQUES.    That's right.    (*To the* JUSTICE.)    I saw him with a
casket.

JUSTICE.    The casket—what was it like ?

JACQUES.    What was what like ?

JUSTICE (*moving in to* L. *of* JACQUES).    The casket.    (*To* HARPA-
GON.)    We'll soon find out whether it was the missing one.    (*To*
JACQUES.)    Well—what was it like ?

JACQUES.    What was it like ?

JUSTICE.    Yes—what was it like ?

JACQUES.    Well, (*he makes a vague gesture with both hands*) it was—
it was like a casket.

JUSTICE. Of course, of course. But I want details. It's *size*—what about that ? Was it large ?

JACQUES (*looking from the* JUSTICE *to* HARPAGON). Er—small.

HARPAGON (*breaking down* R.). Oh, mine was large.

JACQUES (*to* HARPAGON). Oh—of course it was large—if you compare it to a snuff-box. I called it small because I was comparing it to the—town hall.

HARPAGON (*turning*). That's true enough. It would be small if you compared it to the town hall. (*He pauses.*) It sounds very like mine.

JUSTICE (*to* JACQUES). What colour was it ?

JACQUES. Colour ?

JUSTICE. Yes.

JACQUES. I'm not very good at colours.

(HARPAGON *moves in to* R. *of* JACQUES, *the* JUSTICE *moves in to* L. *to him.*)

It's difficult. (*To* HARPAGON.) How would you describe its colour ?

HARPAGON. Me ?

JUSTICE (*shouting suddenly*). Don't answer.

(HARPAGON *and* JACQUES, *startled, clutch each other.*)

JACQUES (*guessing*). A kind of—of red.

HARPAGON. Blue.

JACQUES (*blandly*). That's what I mean, a reddish-blue, or, (*he breaks below* HARPAGON *down* R.) as you might say, a blueish-red.

(*The* JUSTICE *breaks up* C. *to* L. *of the* CLERK.)

HARPAGON. That's right, it's mine, there's no doubt. (*He crosses to the armchair* L.C. *and sits.*) Oh, Valere, Valere ! Who would have thought it ? After this, I can believe I'm capable of robbing myself.

JACQUES (*looking off* R.). Here he comes. (*He runs up* R.) Master, if you want the truth, don't tell him what I said.

(VALERE *enters down* R.)

HARPAGON (*pointing at* VALERE). There he is !

(VALERE *moves below the settee to* C. *The* JUSTICE, *then the* CLERK, *then* JACQUES, *all point accusing fingers at him.*)

The black-hearted scoundrel !

(VALERE *stops in surprise, looks from* HARPAGON *to* JACQUES, *then moves sharply towards the exit up* R. JACQUES *blocks the way.*)

(*He shouts.*) Hi, you ! Come here ! Come here !

(VALERE *turns and moves to* HARPAGON, *in speechless amazement.*
JACQUES *eases behind the settee.*)

Well, what have you to say for yourself ?

VALERE. My dear master . . .

HARPAGON. How dare you call me " my dear " !

VALERE. I beg your pardon ?

HARPAGON. How dare you beg my pardon ! There's only one
thing for you to do now—confess, confess.

(VALERE *stares at him in silence.*)

Oh, how can you stand there and look me in the face, with the
weight of your abominable crime on your conscience ? What a
betrayal ! What treachery ! I take you into my household ; I
trust you above all others ; I treat you as one of the family—and
this is my reward : this infamous, this utterly unspeakable theft.

JACQUES (*easing down* R.). Tsst, tsst, tsst !

(*There is a short pause as* VALERE *takes a step or two down* C., *then
turns, and with his back almost to the audience, faces* HARPAGON.)

VALERE (*quietly*). Master—since, obviously, everything has been
discovered, I'll make no attempt to deny it.

JACQUES (*moving below the settee*). My God ! I've guessed right.

JUSTICE. What's this ? You admit it ?

VALERE (*after a short pause*). How can I do otherwise ?

HARPAGON. You mean—you don't deny it ?

VALERE. Why should I ? For some days past, I've been meaning to discuss it with you.

HARPAGON. Discuss it ?

VALERE. But now that you know, (*he takes a step towards*
HARPAGON) I beg you not to be angry.

HARPAGON. Angry ! Not to be angry ! What d'you expect ?
D'you expect me to throw my arms around your neck and kiss you
on both cheeks ?

VALERE (*moving to* R. *of* HARPAGON *and holding on to the back of
the armchair*). Monsieur Harpagon, that I've done you a great
wrong, I admit.

(*The* CLERK *rises and moves slowly above the settee, writing.*)

HARPAGON. Oh, you do, do you ? You go as far as that ?

VALERE. But, after all, my offence is understandable.

HARPAGON (*rising and breaking down* L.). Understandable ! You
rob me of the most precious thing in all my house . . .

VALERE. I agree, I agree. Of course, I agree. But it isn't as if—
your great treasure had fallen into bad hands.

HARPAGON (*turning*). Bad hands !

VALERE. It isn't as if I'd acted in any spirit of greed. No. From
the very first moment that I entered your house, and my eyes fell—

on the—object of my desire, I've been actuated only by love.

HARPAGON.   Love—of my money !

VALERE.   Oh, Monsieur Harpagon—no, no, no.   I wouldn't have you think that—not for a moment.   After all, what is money ?   I don't want a penny of your money—as long as you let me keep what I've got.

HARPAGON.   Keep what you've got !   (*He moves to* R. *of the armchair.   To the* JUSTICE.)   Did you hear that ?

VALERE.   Master, that of which I robbed you, *you* haven't lost. It's still *yours*.   Nor can it ever again be taken from *me*.

HARPAGON (*crossing below* VALERE *to* L. *of* JACQUES).   I'm going mad !

VALERE (*taking a step down* C. ; *with deep feeling*).   For never, Monsieur Harpagon, never again, in this life—whatever you may say, whatever you may do, can we be parted.   Bound together, as we are, irrevocably—by a mutual passion which consumes, (*he pauses*) and illuminates us both.

HARPAGON.   *He's* mad !   The fear of the gallows has driven him out of his senses.   (*He pauses.*)

(*The* JUSTICE *moves behind the armchair* L.C.)

(*With a sudden rush of fury, he raises his voice to a shout.*)   What have you done with what you have taken ?

VALERE (*looking from the* JUSTICE *to* HARPAGON).   Done, master ?

JUSTICE.   Still in the house ?

VALERE.   Why, yes, of course.

HARPAGON. . Intact ?

VALERE.   Master !

HARPAGON.   You haven't *tampered*, in any way ?

VALERE.   Master, you insult me !   (*He moves sharply in to face* HARPAGON.)   You insult us both !   You insult all three of us !

HARPAGON.   *Three !*

(*The* JUSTICE *moves quickly down* L.)

VALERE.   You insult me ; you insult yourself—and you insult your daughter.

HARPAGON.   What, in God's name, has my daughter to do with it ?

(ELISE, MARIANE *and* FROSINE, *hand in hand, enter up* R., *cross and group up* C., MARIANE *is* R. *and* FROSINE *is* L. *of* ELISE.)

VALERE.   I do assure you, Master, from the depths of my soul, she's in no way to blame.

HARPAGON.   I should hope not, indeed.

VALERE.   From the first, she's been modesty itself.   (*He breaks to* R. *of the armchair.*)   It's taken me all the time since I first came into your house, to gain her consent.

HARPAGON (*moving* C.).   Her consent ?   What consent ?   Her consent to what ?

VALERE.   To the engagement.
HARPAGON.   What engagement ?
VALERE.   *Our* engagement.
HARPAGON.   *Ours ?*   Whose ?
VALERE.   Your daughter's—and mine.
HARPAGON.   My  daughter—and  *you ?*   An  engagement—in
marriage ?
VALERE.   What else ?
HARPAGON (*with a great cry*).   Oh, infamy, infamy, infamy !   (*He
suddenly grabs* ELISE.)   Outrage  upon  outrage !   Wretched  girl !
Wretched, wretched, wretched !   (*He pulls her down* C.)

(ELISE *falls to her knees at* HARPAGON's *feet,* L. *of him and facing* R.
JACQUES *runs to* HARPAGON *and grabs hold of his coat.*   MARIANE
*runs behind* JACQUES *and holds on to him.*   FROSINE *runs and holds
on to* HARPAGON's *left arm.*   The JUSTICE *quickly hides behind the
armchair* L.C.)

(*He stands threateningly over* ELISE.)   I can scarce keep my fingers
from your throat.
VALERE (*falling to his knees,* R. *of the armchair*).   Master !
HARPAGON (*to* ELISE).   I could throttle the life out of you.

(MARIANE, *almost fainting, clings to* JACQUES.)

VALERE.   How can you speak so to your own daughter ?

(JACQUES *turns and supports* MARIANE.)

HARPAGON (*to* ELISE).   Give yourself to a servant, and a thief,
would you ?

(JACQUES *sits* MARIANE *on the settee.*)

(*He crosses below* ELISE *to* R. *of* VALERE.)   Before you're a day older,
you'll be swinging from a gallows.

(FROSINE *moves to* MARIANE *and assists* JACQUES *to bring her round.*
*The* CLERK *leans over the back of the settee and fans* MARIANE *with
his papers.*)

VALERE.   Master, at least *listen* to me.
ELISE (*turning on her knees to face* HARPAGON).   Father, I beg of
you !   (*She raises her clasped hands to him pleadingly.*)   You'll look
with kindlier eyes on my lover, I know you will, when you learn he's
not what you think he is.
HARPAGON (*seizing her hands and throwing her to the floor*).   I know
that already, thank you !   (*He turns and takes a step up* C.)   Justice.
JUSTICE (*still on his knees behind the armchair*).   Yes, Monsieur ?

(VALERE *bends over* ELISE.   MARIANE *rises and* FROSINE *leads her
above, then behind the settee.*   JACQUES *eases below the settee, then
behind it.*)

HARPAGON.   You heard this man confess—

(*The* JUSTICE *crawls above the armchair to* C.)

—on every count ?

JUSTICE (*getting to his feet*).   Yes, Monsieur.

HARPAGON.   Do your duty—arrest him !

(VALERE *and* ELISE *rise to their feet.* ELISE *below* VALERE, *both facing* R.)

JUSTICE (*moving down* C. *to* R. *of* VALERE).   Yes, Monsieur.

VALERE (*with tremendous ferocity*).   Touch me, at your peril.

JUSTICE (*to* HARPAGON ; *in terror*).   I must fetch my men.   (*He moves up* L.)

FROSINE (*glancing off* R.).   Here's a to-do !

ALL.   What ?

FROSINE (*crossing up* L.C.).   He's come to claim his bride.

ALL.   Who ?

FROSINE.   Seigneur Anselm.

ALL.   Anselm ?

FROSINE.   What's to happen now ?

(ELISE *and* VALERE *cross quickly below the settee,* VALERE R. *of* ELISE. MARIANE *eases below* JACQUES, *behind the settee.  The* CLERK *follows* FROSINE *across up* L.   HARPAGON *stands* R. *of the armchair* L.C., *facing up* R.  *The* SEIGNEUR ANSELM *enters up* R.  *He is an up-standing silver-grey-haired elderly man of great distinction.  He pauses for a moment up* R.)

ANSELM (*moving* C.).   My dear Harpagon.   (*He shakes hands with him.*)   What is it ?   What can be the matter ?   You look distraught —beside yourself.

HARPAGON.   So would you be !   (*He points to* VALERE.)   See that fellow there—that one, with crime written all over him ?

(*The* JUSTICE *moves up* C.  *The* CLERK *eases behind the armchair* L.C. FROSINE *crosses below the* JUSTICE, *places herself between* VALERE *and* ELISE, *and keeps* VALERE *at arm's length.*)

He was planning to steal my daughter.   He was planning to steal your wife.   Well—there he stands, self-confessed.   (*He eases a little down* L.)   Take your revenge.

(*There is a pause.*   ANSELM *treats* HARPAGON *with a slightly amused contempt.  He eases a little down* R.C., *then speaks with unruffled dignity.*)

ANSELM.   My good Harpagon, I assure you, I have no intention of marrying any woman against her will—

(FROSINE *sits on the settee, at the* R. *end of it.*)

—and, (*he moves to* ELISE *and takes her hand*) in particular, I would not dream of holding your daughter to any arrangement, (*he kisses* ELISE'S *hand*) if her heart (*he glances at* VALERE) is elsewhere. (*He still holds* ELISE'S *hand and speaks over his shoulder.*) But, for yourself, my dear Harpagon, if you've been wronged—why, to be sure, I'll protect your interests, as if they were my own. (*He gives* ELISE *a slight bow, releases her hand, moves to the armchair* L.C. *and sits.*)

(ELISE *moves in to* L. *of* VALERE.)

HARPAGON.  Well said, well said. (*He moves* C., *points to* ANSELM, *and addresses* VALERE.) The Chief Magistrate of the Town. (*To* ANSELM.) *You* deal with him. (*He moves down* L.) Take over his case—and make it as black against him as you can.

VALERE (*crossing below* ELISE *to* R.C. ; *angrily*).  I must protest !

(MARIANE *moves to* R. *of* ELISE.)

Why should my affection, my love for your daughter be called a crime ?

HARPAGON.  Why—why ! *You*—a rascally servant !

VALERE.  True, in your eyes, I am a servant ; nor can I blame you for that. It was part of my deception.

HARPAGON.  Hark at him !

VALERE (*with growing dignity*).  But I'd have you know, Monsieur Harpagon, I'd have you know—that in myself, I am of gentle, even noble, birth.

(*They all react.* JACQUES *eases up* R. FROSINE *rises and moves behind the settee, at the* R. *end of it. The* JUSTICE *moves behind the* L. *end of the settee. The* CLERK *crosses to* R. *of the* JUSTICE. MARIANE *moves up* R. *of the settee, then above it.*)

HARPAGON (*sitting suddenly on the stool* L.C.).  Rubbish ! Stuff-and-nonsense !

VALERE (*to* HARPAGON ; *indignantly*).  You wrong me, Monsieur, indeed you do. Never would I make *any* claim to which I hadn't *every* right. I'll go further—there's no living *soul* throughout the whole great city of Naples, who couldn't bear witness to the truth of what I'm about to tell you.

ANSELM.  Naples ! Take care, young man. I know Naples.

VALERE.  You know Naples ?

ANSELM.  Every stone of it.

VALERE.  Then you've heard of the Count of Alberti ?

(MARIANE *moves up* C.)

ANSELM (*leaning forward ; completely taken by surprise*).  The Count of Alberti ?

VALERE.  You've heard of him ?

ANSELM.  Why, yes, I've heard of him. Even, I might say, in a way, I knew him.

VALERE.  You *knew* him ?

ANSELM.  No man better.

(*This time it is* VALERE'S *turn to be taken utterly by surprise. For a moment,* ANSELM *and* VALERE *stare at each other, then* HARPAGON *breaks in.*)

HARPAGON.  What's all this ?  What's Naples to do with it ?  What do I care for Count What's-his-name ?  Or any count ?  Or anyone else ?

ANSELM.  Let him alone, good Harpagon, let him alone.  Give him rope ;  and, if he goes on like this, in a few moments he'll be tied in a thousand knots.  (*To* VALERE.)  Well, young man, we're waiting.  What more have you to tell us ?

VALERE.  That the Count of Alberti, of whom you've heard, and whom you profess to have known—was my father.

ANSELM.  Your father !

VALERE.  My father.

(ANSELM *regards* VALERE *for a moment, in utter amazement—then bursts into laughter. The* JUSTICE, FROSINE *and* JACQUES *cross above* MARIANE *and group above the armchair* L.C., *the* JUSTICE *to* L. *of* FROSINE, JACQUES *to* R. *of her.*)

ANSELM (*laughing*).  Really !  This is too fantastic !  You'll have to think of a better story than that.  (*He slaps* HARPAGON'S *right knee and laughs heartily.*)

(*The* CLERK *moves* L. *of the settee and sits at the* R. *end of it.*)

VALERE (*with a step* C. ; *livid with rage*).  Stop that noise !

(*The laugh dies on* ANSELM'S *lips, as if he'd been struck.*)

ANSELM (*after a pause ; almost whispering*).  How dare you speak like that !

VALERE (*angrily*).  How dare you doubt my words !

ANSELM (*rising angrily and taking a step towards* VALERE).  And how dare such a claim pass your lips !

(*The* JUSTICE *moves behind the armchair* L.C., *then down* L.)

Your impudence, your audacity, are beyond bearing.

(HARPAGON *rises.*)

I suppose you made choice of such a parent—one of the wealthiest and noblest men of the city—because you knew he'd been dead some twenty years—and cannot be here, himself, to give you the lie.

VALERE (*stepping to* R. *of* ANSELM).  Sixteen years ago, he was fleeing from the revolution in Naples ;  the ship in which he was making his escape struck on a rock and sank.

(HARPAGON *eases behind the armchair* L.C. *to* R. *of* FROSINE.)

ANSELM (*after a pause*). So ! You know that much. Unfortunately for you, I can add to that. (*He turns to the* JUSTICE.) Olga —his wife, and his two children—his son and daughter ; *his only son*—were with him on that ship ; and perished with him, (*he turns to* VALERE) on that same night.

JUSTICE. Oh !

VALERE (*quietly*). The son was saved. I can remember those moments as if they were now. (*He pauses for a moment, and seems to look into the distance.*)

(*They are all intent on what* VALERE *is to say.*)

My father—the most honoured guest on the ship—was with the captain on his poop ; I had just said good night to my little sister ; my mother had taken her below to bed ; they had just disappeared along the deck. I was standing by the ship's side, gazing down into the passing sea, in charge of a family servant. My hand was in his. (*He pauses.*) Below me, stars danced in the black water, above they filled the sky—the night was very still. Only the lap and swish of the sea, and the slow creaking of the ship—then a sudden grinding crash—and I found myself in the sea. I struck out ; I felt an arm round me—it was the old servant ; he supported me ; gained a piece of wreckage ; pulled me up beside him ; and on it we drifted till morning. And when the dawn came, there was no sign of the ship, nor of any survivors. But before the next night fell we were picked up by a boat on its way to Spain. (*He pauses.*) Only recently, as I was at length making my way back to my native city, I saw Elise. (*He turns and moves in to* L. *of* ELISE.) From that moment, where she was, was home. (*He turns, takes a step or two up* R.C. *and with his back to the audience, looks at* HARPAGON.) I took service with her father, so as never to leave her side again.

MARIANE (*moving down* C. *a little and facing* VALERE). This old family servant whom you spoke of, and in whose charge you were— was his name—Pedro ?

(ANSELM *looks startled.*)

VALERE. Why, yes of course ! Old Pedro ! But how d'you know ? How can you possibly know ?

MARIANE. I, and my mother, had hardly reached our cabin when the ship struck. (*She faces* ANSELM *and the group behind the arm-chair* L.C.) She seized me up, and was thrown into the sea, clasping me in her arms. Some sailors dragged us on to a raft ; for days and nights we were on it ; and were rescued by some fishing boats near to the coast of Africa. (*She turns to* VALERE.) How often have I heard it from my mother. My father on the poop with the captain—

(*The* CLERK *rises and with tears in his eyes, moves below the settee, then behind it.*)

—my brother on the deck with old Pedro.

VALERE. Your brother ? (*He takes* MARIANE *in his arms and kisses her.*)

(*The* CLERK, *wiping his eyes, moves above the settee.*)

ANSELM (*after a pause ; moving to* L. *of* VALERE *and* MARIANE). Have you any further proof of this strange story, in which you so strangely agree ?

(ELISE *draws* VALERE'S *attention to the ring he is wearing.*)

VALERE (*holding out his hand to* ANSELM). My father's ring. He gave it to Pedro ; and, on his death-bed, old Pedro gave it back to me.

(ANSELM *bends for a moment over* VALERE'S *outstretched hand to look at the ring, then stands upright.*)

ANSELM. The ways of God are mysterious. How well I remember giving that ring to old Pedro.

VALERE. You ?

ANSELM. I, too, was saved ! With the captain, I found myself in a small boat, but with a company of sailors whose one thought was home. They resisted every command, every entreaty to remain, even for a moment, on the scene of the wreck. They turned the boat towards home, and their oars dipped and pulled, pulled and dipped, till we beached on the shores of Italy. (*He pauses.*) Caring little whether I lived or died, I returned to Naples where I found my palace and my estates untouched—and there I have lived for sixteen years, mourning the loss of my wife and children. I came here under an assumed name to start life anew ; and here, miracle of miracles, I find . . .

(MARIANE *runs to* ANSELM, *throws her arms around his neck and kisses him.* VALERE *clasps* ANSELM'S *hand, then reaches for* ELISE *and draws her to him.* MARIANE *breaks up* C.)

HARPAGON (*moving above the armchair* L.C., *then to* R. *of it and* L. *of* ANSELM). Here—hi—what's going on ? Let me get hold of things—the right end of the stick. Are you saying this man is your son ?

(*The* JUSTICE *moves up* L.)

ANSELM (*taking hold of* VALERE'S *left hand*). I am.

HARPAGON. Then I hold you responsible for all the money he's stolen from me—ten thousand crowns.

(ELISE *breaks down* R.)

ANSELM. Stolen money—my son ?

VALERE. *I* steal your money ?

HARPAGON (*moving below the armchair* L.C.). Well, you told me yourself . . .

VALERE. *I* told you ?

HARPAGON. Yes—so did Jacques.

JACQUES (*moving quickly to* R. *of* VALERE). *Me ?*

HARPAGON. Yes, you.

VALERE (*turning to* JACQUES *and drawing him down* C. ; *quietly*). You told Monsieur Harpagon that I'd stolen his money ? What were you thinking about ? What have you to say for yourself ?

(HARPAGON *sits on the stool* L.C.)

JACQUES. Nothing ! I say nothing. (*He pauses and kneels at* VALERE'S *feet.*) Oh, good Monsieur Valere, it was you yourself taught me that truth was no good.

(LA FLECHE *enters up* L.)

Now I've found out for myself that lies are no better—so henceforth for the rest of my life I keep silent, I say nothing.

(LA FLECHE *and* FROSINE *confer in whispers behind the armchair* L.C. JACQUES *rises and eases behind the settee.*)

HARPAGON (*after a pause*). But this is terrible ! If you didn't take my money, who did ? I want my treasure back ! I want—

FROSINE. You shall have your treasure back.

HARPAGON. —my money back.

LA FLECHE (*moving above the armchair to* C.). On one condition.

HARPAGON (*turning to face* LA FLECHE). A condition ?

FROSINE (*aside*). Bait your hook with a man's weakness and watch the poor fish bite. (*She calls.*) Cleante !

ELISE (*turning and calling off* R.). Cleante !

LA FLECHE (*calling*). Master Cleante !

(CLEANTE *enters down* R. *and moves* C. FROSINE *takes the* JUSTICE'S *hand and leads him down* L. LA FLECHE *eases below the settee to* R. *of* ELISE.)

CLEANTE. It's all right, dear Father. I know where it is.

(VALERE *eases to* L. *of* ELISE.)

HARPAGON. You know ?

CLEANTE. Yes, if you will give me Mariane. Now, make up your mind.

(MARIANE *moves to* R. *of* CLEANTE.)

HARPAGON. My casket—has it been opened ?

CLEANTE. Yes.

HARPAGON. And the money gone ?

CLEANTE. No, not a piece.

HARPAGON. How d'you know ?

CLEANTE (*holding* MARIANE'S *left hand in his right*).   You shall see for yourself—

(MARIANE *and* CLEANTE *kneel to* HARPAGON, CLEANTE *above* MARIANE.)

—the moment after you say—yes.

MARIANE (*to* CLEANTE).   But, my dearest, your father's consent is no longer enough—for Heaven, in its great goodness, has restored me a father, too.

ANSELM (*moving to* R. *of* MARIANE *and helping her to rise*).   And I'm quite sure Heaven hasn't restored you a father to forbid you to marry the man you love.   (*He kisses her.*)

(CLEANTE *rises.*)

(*Between* MARIANE *and* VALERE.)   So come, my dear Harpagon, agree, as I do, to this double marriage—your son to my daughter—

(CLEANTE *bows,* MARIANE *curtsies.*)

—and your daughter to my son.

(VALERE *bows,* ELISE *curtsies.*   CLEANTE *and* MARIANE, *close together, ease a little up* L.C.   VALERE *turns to* ELISE.)

HARPAGON (*crossing to* ANSELM *and tugging his coat*).   I haven't got any money to give 'em.

ANSELM.   Then it's fortunate I have.

HARPAGON.   I shall want a new coat for the wedding—will you buy me a new coat ?

ANSELM.   With all my heart.

JUSTICE (*moving below the armchair* L.C.).   And who's going to pay *me* ?

(SIMON *enters up* L.)

FROSINE.   And me ?
CLERK.   And me ?
LA FLECHE.   And me ?
SIMON.   And me ?

(LA FLECHE *exits down* R.)

HARPAGON (*to the* JUSTICE).   You !   What do you want paying for ?   (*He moves to* C.)   Hang Master Jacques for a false witness, and we'll think about it.   (*He sits on the* CLERK'S *stool up* C.)

JUSTICE.   Irregular !

JACQUES.   Dear, oh dear !   Beaten for telling the truth, hanged for telling lies, and my beautiful sucking pig burned to a cinder.

ANSELM (*easing down* L.C.).   In which case, I propose we all repair to *my* house—where my chef will provide a wedding feast.

(*They all cheer.*)

Let the young couples lead the way.

VALERE (*taking* ELISE *by the hand*).　Elise.

(*They run hand in hand up* L. *of the settee to up* R.)

CLEANTE (*taking* MARIANE *by the hand*).　Mariane.

(*They run to* VALERE *and* ELISE, *and the four of them hand in hand dance off merrily up* R.　*They are followed off by the* CLERK *and* SIMON.　JACQUES *exits down* R.　FROSINE *takes hold of the* JUSTICE'S *hand, leads him across and they exit down* R., *leaving* ANSELM *alone with* HARPAGON.)

ANSELM (*moving down* R.).　Come along, old Harpagon, come along.

(*He exits down* R.　HARPAGON *rises despondently and moves down* R.　*As he is about to exit,* LA FLECHE *enters down* L.　*He has the casket clasped in his arms.　He moves* C. *and puts the casket down on the floor with a bang.*　HARPAGON *turns, startled, and sees the casket.*)

HARPAGON (*with a loud screech*).　Aaaah !　(*He rushes to the casket.*)

(LA FLECHE, *scared, turns and runs hurriedly off* L.)

(*He falls on his knees beside the casket and embraces it.*)　Oh, my own !　My treasure !　My precious !　(*He opens the casket.*)　Are you all there ?　Have you been ravaged ?　No—doesn't look like it.　But how can I tell ?　They may have taken some from the bottom.　Better find out.　(*He picks out a handful of coins and starts to count.*)　One—two—three . . .　(*He hesitates, looks off* R., *then resumes counting.*)

*The* CURTAIN *falls, but rises almost at once.*　HARPAGON *is surrounded by little piles of gold coins, and still counting furiously.*

**CURTAIN**

# FURNITURE AND PROPERTY LIST

Wing ____  Settee  Arm chair Stool  Wing

*Throughout the play :*
*On Stage.*—Settee.
           Armchair.
           Stool.
           Chandeliers.
           Carpet on floor.

## ACT I

### SCENE 1

*Personal.*—HARPAGON : Stick.   Snuff box with snuff.
          ELISE : Fan.

### SCENE 2

*Personal.*—HARPAGON : Watch.  Purse, *in it :* coins.
          LA FLECHE : Document.
          SIMON : Document.
          FROSINE : Bundle of receipts.  Handbag, *in it :* mirror, pencil,
                paper.

## ACT II

### SCENE 1

*Off Stage.*—Party notes.  (HARPAGON.)
          Chef's cap and apron.  (JACQUES.)
          Slate and pencil.  (JACQUES.)
          Coachman's top hat and whip.  (JACQUES.)
          Small chest, *in it :* coins.
*Personal.*—HARPAGON : Spectacles.  Ring.  Dirty khaki handkerchief.
          FROSINE : Fan.  Handbag.
          MARIANE : Fan.
          ELISE : Fan.
          CLEANTE : Coin.

### SCENE 2

*Off Stage.*—Folding stool.  (CLERK.)
*Personal.*—CLERK : Note-book.  Pencil.  Sheaf of papers.
          JACQUES : Butcher's knife and steel.
          VALERE : Ring.

Printed in Great Britain by Redwood Books,
Trowbridge, Wiltshire